MARQUIS SAINT GERMAIN DER WUNDERMANN.

Original Gemälde im Besitze der Marquise von Urfé
1783 in Kupfer gestochen von N. Thomas in Paris.
Folio seltenes Blatt

THE COMTE DE ST. GERMAIN
THE SECRET OF KINGS

by

I. COOPER-OAKLEY

THEOSOPHICAL PUBLISHING HOUSE LTD
68 Great Russell Street London WC1B 3BU

Adyar, Madras
India

Wheaton, Illinois
USA

First edition	.	.	.	.	1912
Reprinted		.	.	.	1927
Reprinted		.	.	.	1985

ISBN 0 7229 5146 9

PRINTED IN GREAT BRITAIN BY WHITSTABLE LITHO LTD.,
WHITSTABLE, KENT

DEDICATED TO

THE GREAT SOUL

WHO IN THE STRUGGLES OF THE EIGHTEENTH

CENTURY WORKED

SUFFERED AND TRIUMPHED

PUBLISHERS' NOTE

This book, originally published in 1912 by " Ars Regia " of Milan, is being re-issued because it has become so rare as to reach prohibitive prices, while it is constantly needed by students of the history of occultism. Certain difficulties, however, have had to be faced. The author is dead and no authoritative revision is therefore possible. The original text was set up by Italian compositors whose work was obviously not carefully corrected. The result is that it teems with errors of spelling and punctuation. In addition to this certain of the documents contained were evidently translated into English by foreigners and the translations were not revised. This results at times in some very quaint English. Further, the apparent lack of opportunity of correcting proofs has also caused a certain lack of uniformity as to the precise spelling of names, titles of books, form of references and the like.

While none of these defects can be said to detract from the interest or value of the book, to perpetuate them in a new issue seemed inadvisable. On the other hand, short of many months or even years of work by an editor qualified to deal with the material, who is not easily to be found, the kind of revision, rearrangement and amplification which should at some time be undertaken is impossible. We have therefore made only such corrections as are unquestionable; for example, in punctuation, spelling, uniformity (where the correct form is known), grammar (where the sense is absolutely unaltered) ; otherwise the text has been left precisely as it first appeared. For the illustrations blocks have had to be made from the badly printed pages of the original. We have been able by careful workmanship to improve on them, but we disclaim any idea of their being as satisfactory as if we could have worked from the original documents, pictures and photographs.

CONTENTS

CHAPTER I.

The theories of his birth—High connections—The friend of kings and princes—Various titles—Supposed Prince Ragoczy—Historic traces—At the Court at Anspach—Friend of the Orloffs—Moral character given by Prince Charles of Hesse.

CHAPTER II.

The Comte de St. Germain at Venice in 1710 and the Countess de Georgy—Letter to the British Museum in 1733 from the Hague—From 1737 to 1742 in Persia—In England in 1745—In Vienna in 1746—In 1755 in India—In 1757 comes to Paris —In 1760 at The Hague—In St. Petersburg in 1762—In Brussels in 1763—Starting new experiments in manufactories—In 1760 in Venice—News from an Italian Newspaper for 1770—M. de St. Germain at Leghorn—In Paris again in 1774— At Triesdorf in 1776—At Leipzig in 1777—Testimony of high character by contemporary writers.

Chapter III.

Chapter IV.

Chapter V.

Chapter VI.

Chapter VII.

Chapter VIII.

Appendix I.

Appendix II.

Appendix III.

LIST OF ILLUSTRATIONS

FOREWORD

Mrs. Cooper-Oakley's painstaking research is so well known, and so highly appreciated among students, that it is not necessary for me to recommend her work. She has travelled far and wide over Europe, visiting famous libraries, in order to collect, with long perseverance and unwearied exertion, the materials which we read at our ease, in comfortable armchairs, with our feet on the fender. So we owe her our attention and our gratitude.

The great Occultist and Brother of the White Lodge, fragments of whose life are herein given, was the greatest force behind the intellectual reforming movement which received its death-blow in the outbreak of the French Revolution. Phoenix-like, it has re-arisen, and it re-appeared in the 19th century as the Theosophical Society, of which this great Brother is one of the recognised Leaders. Still living in the same body the perennial youth of which astonished the observers of the 18th century, He has fulfilled the prophecy made to Mme. d'Adhémar that He would show Himself again a century after His farewell to her, and, in the growing spiritual movement which is seen around us on every side, He will be one of the acknowledged Chiefs. Profoundly interesting, therefore, must be every detail that can be gathered of His eighteenth century life, and much is gathered here.

ANNIE BESANT

President of the Theosophical Society

LONDON, 1911

PREFACE

I have thought it better, in preparing the first part of the monograph on the Life of the Comte de St. Germain, to reprint the articles which were published in 1897 in the " Theosophical Review " with some additional matter, rather than rewrite an entirely new book, since to many persons those magazine articles are not easily accessible.

Perhaps some critics may think that there is too much quoted matter ; this I have done on purpose in order that the opinions of those persons who were in actual contact with the Comte de St. Germain may be considered, rather than my own. In the eighteenth century every one of any education kept a diary, and in these diaries we get a living picture of the period ; this is very decidely the case in the Memoirs of Madame d'Adhémar.

It has been suggested, by one writer in the Nineteenth Century, that these Memoirs are apocryphal. I do not think so, as the present Comtesse d'Adhémar informed me that they have documents about the Comte de St. Germain in their possesion.

In the second part of this study there is much additional political material ; unfortunately, in the

English Record Office, all the ciphers which were between the written lines were carefully erased, before the papers were consigned to me. Evidently there was some mystery about this political work which is even now not to be made public.

I take this opportunity of thanking the many friends, and specially Mon. G. Mallet, who have helped me with the arduous work of copying and translating. Without their valuable help this study could not have been printed.

I am now collecting more material which will form the second part of this monograph when complete.

ISABEL COOPER-OAKLEY

LONDON, 1911

Bible, la Preuve en est, qu'il n'y a absolument qu'une seule et unique Marque de Ponctuation, savoir le Point rond, dans l'Endroit même du Livre où cette Ponctuation est divisée par l'Auteur en coma ou Point avec Virgule au dessus, Colum ou Point sans Virgule, et Periodus en Point avec Virgule au dessous: au lieu que, dans la Bible de 1462, on voit par-tout le Point, les deux Points, le Point interrogant, &c. Il est donc visible que cette Edition est antérieure de quelques Années, & faite sans doute avant le Procès de ces 3 Imprimeurs jugé en 1455, et avant qu'ils missent des Dates à leurs Editions; caque Fust et Schoiffer, séparés de Guttemberg, ne firent qu'en 1457 dans le Psautier Latin, la plus ancienne de toutes les Editions Datées. Voilà pour l'Histoire de cette Edition.

Quant à l'Exemplaire que j'ai, il est parfaitement bien conservé, et relié en Bois couvert de Peau de Truie, semé de Fleurs de Lis, cantonnées chacune de quatre Rosettes, et renfermées dans des Lozanges formées par de triples Lignes se croisant les unes les autres de Biais, de toute la Hauteur du Volume, et renfermées elles-mêmes dans un Cadre ou Bordure de Dragons, divisés par une longue Bande de courant en Zig-Zag; &, sur cette Couverture, il y avoit autrefois des Coins & des Bossettes, dont les Marques se distinguent très bien encore. Il est de plus antiqué sur la Tranche; et lavé et réglé, non seulement à l'ordinaire autour de chaque Page, mais extraordinairement sous chaque Ligne: &, outre que les grandes Lettres qui commencent chacun des Traittés et Chapitres sont enjolivées de Fleurons & Feuillages peints en Vermillon et en Azur, toutes celles du commencement de chaque Article de ce Dictionaire, ce qui va à un Nombre infini, sont des mêmes Couleurs alternativement, depuis le Commencement jusqu'à la fin. Ce sont deux Tomes in folio, qui font un Volume d'une Grandeur & Grosseur extraordinaire. On n'y voit rien d'écrit à la main, come dans la plûpart des vieux Livres, qui en sont fort défigurés.

Tel est, Monsieur, le Livre, dont j'ai cru devoir me donner l'Honneur de vous écrire, & dont je ne me serois point avisé de vous importuner, si ce n'étoit une Piéce extraordinaire, très rare, & tout-à-fait digne d'occuper une Place dans une Bibliothèque aussi utile & aussi renommée que la Vôtre. Afin que Vous puissiés la faire examiner par quelque Personne de Confiance ici, je prendrai la liberté de joindre à tout ceci mon Adresse, après vous avoir assuré très humblement, du Respect avec lequel je suis,

+ Elle ne se trouve nulle part ailleurs qu'à Ste Genneviève de Paris

Monsieur,

A la Haye, ce 22. Nov.bre 1735.

Votre très humble & très obéissant Serviteur
P. M. de St Germain, chez la Veuve Vincent, sur le Nieuwe-Have, in de Tuyn-Laan.

Monfieur

Connoiffant depuis longtems votre Goût pour les livres rares, & le Soin que vous prenez d'en enrichir continuellement votre belle & nombreuse Bibliotheque, j'ai cru que je vous ferois plaifir de vous parler d'une des plus rares & des plus fingulieres qu'on connoiffe; puifque c'eft un Exemplaire de la feconde de toutes les Editions du Monde faites avec des Caracteres mobiles. La premiere, comme vous le favez fans doute, eft une <u>Bible Latine</u>, dont Trithéme parle fous l'Année 1450 de fes <u>Annales Hirfaugienfes</u>, et aprés lui Mr. Chevillier, Maittaire, & quantité d'autres. La feconde, qui eft celle dont il s'agit, & que je puis vous prouver, eft un <u>Catholicon Joannis Januenfis</u>, inconnu à tous les Bibliothecaires, excepté les feuls Peres Quetif & Echard, qui en parlent ainfi dans leurs <u>Scriptures Ordinis Prædicatorum recenfiti</u>, Tom. I, pag. 462, ce que vous pourrez verifier. Altera (la premiere étoit une Edition en Planches de Bois du même Livre, qui fut le 1er Ouvrage réel de Guttemberg, Fust, & Schoiffer, et auquel fucceda la <u>Bible Latine</u> en Caracteres mobiles:) altera en Arte Typographica and 1460 tum perfectâ, tamen absque Numeris, Signaturis, Reclamationibus, Anno, Loco, Nomine Typotheta, abfque Litteris etiam initialibus, quæ omnes adita et picta: quam Moguntiæ prodiffe conficiunt. Extat ejufce Exemplaar Parifiis, in Genovefirâ Bibliothecâ, in folio maximo, Chartâ Regiâ.

L'Exemplaire que j'ai eft tout femblable à celui-là; et il n'y a nul Doute, qu'il ne foit de Mayence, et de l'Imprimerie des trois premiers Imprimeurs de cette <u>Bible</u> & du Monde, puifque le Papier fur lequel il eft imprimé porte les Mêmes Marques que celui fur lequel Schoiffer feul imprima fon <u>Decretum Gratiani</u> en 1472. Le Caractere eft tout femblable pour la Forme, mais un peu plus petit, que celui de la <u>Bible Latine de 1462</u>; et fes Pages font beaucoup plus hautes et plus larges, chaque colonne aiant 65 lignes au lieu que celles de la <u>Bible</u> n'en ont que quarante-huit. Que ce <u>Catholicon</u> foit plus ancien que

celle

THE COMTE DE ST. GERMAIN

CHAPTER I

MYSTIC AND PHILOSOPHER

HE was, perhaps, one of the greatest philosophers who ever lived. The friend of humanity, wishing for money only that he might give to the poor, a friend to animals, his heart was concerned only with the happiness of others.—*Mémoires de Mon Temps*, p. 135. S. A. LE LANDGRAVE CHARLES, PRINCE DE HESSE. (Copenhagen, 1861.)

DURING the last quarter of every hundred years an attempt is made by those Masters, of whom I have spoken, to help on the spiritual progress of Humanity. Towards the close of each century you will invariably find that an outpouring or upheaval of spirituality—or call it mysticism if you prefer—has taken place. Some one or more persons have appeared in the world as their agents, and a greater or less amount of occult knowledge or teaching has been given out.—*The Key to Theosophy* (p. 194). H. P. BLAVATSKY.

THE Comte de St. Germain was certainly the greatest Oriental Adept Europe has seen during the last centuries.— *Theosophical Glossary*, H. P. BLAVATSKY.

AMONG the strange mysterious beings, with which the eighteenth century was so richly dowered, no one has commanded more universal comment and attention than the mystic who was known by the name of the Comte de St. Germain. A hero of romance ; a charlatan ; a swindler and an adventurer ; rich and varied were the names

S.G.   B that showered freely upon him. Hated by the many, loved and reverenced by the few, time has not yet lifted the veil which screened his true mission from the vulgar speculators of the period. Then, as now, the occultist was dubbed charlatan by the ignorant ; only some men and women here and there realised the power of which he stood possessed. The friend and councillor of kings and princes, an enemy to ministers who were skilled in deception, he brought his great knowledge to help the West, to stave off in some small measure the storm clouds that were gathering so thickly around some nations. Alas ! his words of warning fell on deafened ears, and his advice went all unheeded.

Looking back from this distance of time it will be of interest to many students of mysticism to trace the life, so far as it may yet be told, of this great occultist. Sketches are to be found here and there from various writers, mostly antagonistic, but no coherent detailed account of his life has yet appeared. This is very largely owing to the fact that the most interesting and important work, done by M. de St. Germain, lies buried in the secret archives of many princely and noble families. With this fact we have become acquainted during the careful investigations which we have been making on the subject. Where the archives are situated we have also learned, but we have not yet in all cases received permission to make the necessary researches.

It must be borne in mind that the Comte de St. Germain, alchemist and mystic, does not belong to the French family of St. Germain, from which descended Count Robert de St. Germain; the latter was born in the year 1708, at Lons-le-Saulnier, was first a Jesuit, and entered later in turn the French, Palatine, and Russian military services; he became Danish Minister of War under Count Struensee, then re-entered the French service, and at the beginning of the reign of Louis XVI., he tried, as Minister of War, to introduce various changes into the French army; these raised a violent storm of indignation; he was disgraced by the king and finally died in 1778. He is so often confounded with his mystic and philosophic namesake, that for the sake of clearing up the ignorance that prevails on the matter it is well to give these brief details, showing the difference between the two men; unfortunately the disgrace into which the soldier fell is but too often attributed to the mystic, to whom we will now turn our entire attention.

That M. de St. Germain had intimate relations with many high persons in various countries is quite undeniable, the testimony on this point being overwhelming. That such relations should cause jealousy and unkindly speculation is unfortunately not rare in any century. Let us, however, see what some of these princely friends say. When questioned by the Herzog Karl August as to the supernatural age of this mystic, the Landgraf von Hessen-Phillips-Barchfeld replied : " We cannot speak with certainty on that point ; the fact is the Count is acquainted with details about which only contemporaries of that period could give us information ; it is now the fashion in Cassel to listen respectfully to his statements and not to be astonished at anything. The Count is known not to be an importunate sycophant ; he is a man of good society to whom all are pleased to attach themselves. . . . . He at all events stands in close relation with many men of considerable importance, and exercises an incomprehensible influence on others. My cousin the Landgraf Karl von Hessen is much attached to him ; they are eager Freemasons, and work together at all sorts of hidden arts. . . . . He is supposed to have intercourse with ghosts and supernatural beings, who appear at his call." [1]

Herr Mauvillon, in spite of his personal prejudice against M. de St. Germain, is obliged to acknowledge the feeling of the Duke towards

[1] AKSAKOF, A., *Psychische Studien, Monatliche Zeitschrift,* xii., p. 430. Leipzig, 1885.

the great alchemist. For on his supposed death being mentioned in the Brunswick newspaper of the period, wherein M. de St. Germain was spoken of as " a man of learning," " a lover of truth," " devoted to the good " and " a hater of baseness and deception," the Duke himself wrote to the editor, expressing his approbation of the announcement.[1]

In France M. de St. Germain appears to have been under the personal care, and enjoying the affection of Louis XV., who repeatedly declared that he would not tolerate any mockery of the Count, who was of high birth. It was this affection and protection that caused the Prime Minister, the Duc de Choiseul, to become a bitter enemy of the mystic, although he was at one time friendly to him, since the Baron de Gleichen in his memoirs says : " M. de St. Germain frequented the house of M. de Choiseul, and was well received there." [2]

The same writer, who later became one of his devoted students, testifies to the fact that M. de St. Germain ate no meat, drank no wine, and lived according to a strict *régime*. Louis XV. gave him a suite of rooms in the royal Château de Chambord, and he constantly spent

[1] MAUVILLON, J., *Geschichte Ferdinands, Herzog von Braunschweig-Luneberg*, ii., p. 479. Leipzig, 1794.
[2] GLEICHEN (E. H. Baron de), *Souvenirs*, Paris, 1868, p. 126.

whole evenings at Versailles with the King and the royal family.

One of the chief difficulties we find in tracing his history consists in the constant changes of name and title, a proceeding which seems to have aroused much antagonism and no little doubt. This fact should not, however, have made the public (of the period) dislike him, for it appears to have been the practice of persons of position, who did not wish to attract vulgar curiosity; thus, for instance, we have the Duc de Medici travelling in the years 1698 and 1700 under the name of the Conte di Siena. The Graf Marcolini, when he went from Dresden to Leipzig to meet M. de St. Germain, adopted another name. The Kur-Prinz Friedrich-Christian von Sachsen travelled in Italy from 1738 to 1740, under the name Comte Lausitz. Nearly all the members of the royal families in every country, during the last century, and even in this, adopted the same practice; but when M. de St. Germain did so, we have all the small writers of that period and later calling him an adventurer and a charlatan for what appears to have been, practically, a custom of the time.

Let us now make a list of these names and titles, bearing in mind that they cover a period of time dating from 1710 to 1822. The first date is mentioned by Baron de Gleichen, who says:

" I have heard Rameau and an old relative of a French ambassador at Venice testify to having known M. de St. Germain in 1710, when he had the appearance of a man of fifty years of age." [1] The second date is mentioned by Mme. d'Adhémar in her most interesting *Souvenirs sur Marie Antoinette*.[2] During this time we have M. de St. Germain as the Marquis de Montferrat, Comte Bellamarre or Aymar at Venice, Chevalier Schoening at Pisa, Chevalier Weldon at Milan and Leipzig, Comte Soltikoff at Genoa and Leghorn, Graf Tzarogy at Schwalbach and Triesdorf, Prinz Ragoczy at Dresden, and Comte de St. Germain at Paris, the Hague, London, and St. Petersburg. No doubt all these varied changes gave ample scope and much material for curious speculations.

A few words may fitly here be said about his personal appearance and education. From one contemporary writer we get the following sketch :—

" He looked about fifty, is neither stout nor thin, has a fine intellectual countenance, dresses very simply, but with taste ; he wears the finest diamonds on snuff-box, watch and buckles. Much of the mystery with which he is surrounded is

[1] GLEICHEN, *op. cit.*, p. 127.

[2] D'ADHÉMAR (La Comtesse), *Souvenirs sur Marie Antoinette, Archiduchesse d'Autriche, Reine de France, et sur la Cour de Versaille*, Paris, 1836.

owing to his princely liberaltity." Another writer, who knew him when at Anspach, says : " He always dined alone and very simply ; his wants were extremely few ; it was impossible while at Anspach to persuade him to dine at the Prince's table."

M. de St. Germain appears to have been very highly educated. According to Karl von Weber,[1] " he spoke German, English, Italian, Portuguese and Spanish very well, and French with a Piedmontese accent."

It was almost universally accorded that he had a charming grace and courtliness of manner. He displayed, moreover, in society, a great variety of gifts, played several musical instruments excellently, and sometimes showed facilities and powers which bordered on the mysterious and incomprehensible. For example, one day he had dictated to him the first twenty verses of a poem, and wrote them simultaneously with both hands on two separate sheets of paper — no one present could distinguish one sheet from the other.

In order to arrive at some orderly sequence, it will be well to divide our material into three parts :—

[1] WEBER (Dr. Carl von), *Aus vier Jahrhunderten. Mittheilungen aus dem Haupt-Staats-Archive, Zu Dresden,* i., p. 312. Tauchnitz, Leipzig, 1857.

i. Theories about his birth and character, with personal details, some of which we have briefly noticed.

ii. His travels and knowledge.

iii. His political and mystical work.

Beginning, then, with our first division, the theories about his birth and nationality are many and various ; and different authors, according to their prejudices, trace his descent from prince or tax-gatherer, apparently as fancy dictates. Thus, among other parentages, we find him supposed to be descended from :—

1. The widow of Charles II. (King of Spain)—the father a Madrid banker.

2. A Portuguese Jew.

3. An Alsatian Jew.

4. A tax-gatherer in Rotondo.

5. King of Portugal (natural son).

6. Franz-Leopold, Prince Ragoczy, of Transylvania.

This last seems to have been the correct view, according to the most reliable sources that have been found, and other information to which we have had access on this point.

This theory is also held by Georg Hezekiel in his *Abenteuerliche Gesellen*, i., 35, Berlin, 1862. Karl von Weber (*op. cit.*, i., 318) also says that M. de St. Germain openly appeared in Leipzig in 1777 as Prince Ragoczy, and that he was

often known as the Graf Tzarogy, which latter
is merely an anagram for Ragotzy (Ragoczy).
This last fact we have verified in another interesting set of articles, to which we shall refer later,
written by a person who knew him at Anspach
under the name Tzarogy. Another writer
remarks : " His real origin would, perhaps,
if revealed, have compromised important persons." And this is the conclusion to which, after
careful investigation, we have also come. Prince
Karl of Hesse,[1] writing of M. de St. Germain,
says :—

" Some curiosity may be felt as to his history ;
I will trace it with the utmost truthfulness,
according to his own words, adding any necessary
explanations. He told me that he was eighty-eight
years of age when he came here, and that he
was the son of Prince Ragoczy [2] of Transylvania
by his first wife, a Tékéli. He was placed, when
quite young, under the care of the last Duc de
Medici (Gian Gastone), who made him sleep
while still a child in his own room. When M.
de St. Germain learned that his two brothers,
sons of the Princess of Hesse-Wahnfried (Rhein-
fels), had become subject to the Emperor Charles

[1] HESSE-CASSEL (Karl, Prinz de), *Mémoires de Mon Temps*,
p. 133. Copenhagen, 1861.

[2] Rágóczy is the German spelling of this name. In
Hungary it is written Rákóczy.

VI., and had received the titles and names of St. Karl and St. Elizabeth, he said to himself : ' Very well, I will call myself Sanctus Germano, the Holy Brother.' I cannot in truth guarantee his birth, but that he was tremendously protected by the Duc de Medici I have learnt from another source."

Another well-known writer speaks on the same point, an author, moreover, who had access to the valuable Milan archives ; we refer to the late Cæsare Cantù, librarian of the great library in Milan, who in his historical work, *Illustri Italiani*, ii., 18, says : " The Marquis of San Germano appears to have been the son of Prince Ragotzy (Ragoczy) of Transylvania ; he was also much in Italy ; much is recounted of his travels in Italy and in Spain ; he was greatly protected by the last Grand Duke of Tuscany, who had educated him." It has been said that M. de St. Germain was educated at the University of Siena ; Mme. de Genlis in her *Mémoires* mentions having heard of him in Siena during a visit that she paid to that town.

The whole life of M. de St. Germain seems to have been more or less shadowed by the political troubles and struggles of his father.

In order to understand this we must take a brief survey of his family history, a survey which will moreover give us some clues, helping us to unravel the tangled web of mysterious elements which surrounded the life and work of the great occultist.

Few pages of history are more deeply scored with sorrow, suffering and impotent struggle than those which tell the life story of the efforts of one Ragoczy after another to preserve the freedom of their principality, and to save it from being swallowed up by the rapidly growing Austrian Empire under the influence of the Roman Church. In an old German book, *Genealogische Archivarius aus dem Jahr* 1734, pp. 409, 410, 438, Leipzig, a sketch is given, on the death of Prince Ragoczy, of his family, his antecedents and descendants, from which we will quote some leading facts : Francis Leopold Racozi, or Rakoczy, according to the later spelling — the father of the famous mystic — made ineffectual efforts to regain his throne, the principality of Siebenbürgen. The Ragoczy property was wealthy and valuable, and Prince Francis, grandfather of the mystic of whom we are writing, had lost his life in a hopeless struggle to retain his freedom ; on his death, his widow and children were seized by the Austrian Emperor, and hence the son, Francis Leopold, was brought up at the Court of Vienna. As our informant says : " The widowed Princess (who had remarried Graf Tékéli) was forced to hand over her children with their properties to the Emperor, who said he would become their guardian and be responsible for their education." This arrangement was made in March, 1688. When, however, Prince Francis came of age, his properties, with many restrictions and limitations, were given back to him by the Emperor of Austria. In 1694 this Prince Ragoczy married at Köln-am-Rhein, Charlotte Amalia, daughter of the Landgraf Karl von Hesse-Wahnfried (of the line of Rhein-fels). Of this marriage there were three children, Joseph, George and Charlotte. Almost immediately after this period Prince Ragoczy began to lead the conspiracies of his noblemen against the Austrian Empire, with the object of regaining his independent power. The history of the struggle is most interesting in every way, and singularly pathetic. The Prince was defeated and all his properties were confiscated. The sons had to give up the name of Ragoczy, and to take the titles of St. Carlo and St. Elizabeth.

Let us notice what Hezekiel [1] has to say on this point, for he has made some very careful investigations on the subject : " We are, in fact, inclined to think the Comte de St. Germain was the younger son of the Prince Franz-Leopold Ragoczy and the Princess Charlotte Amalia of Hesse-Wahnfried. Franz-Leopold was married

[1] *Op. cit.*, i., 45.

in 1694, and by this marriage he had two sons, who were taken prisoners by the Austrians and brought up as Roman Catholics ; they were also forced to give up the dreaded name of Ragoczy. The eldest son, calling himself the Marquis of San Carlo, escaped from Vienna in 1734. In this year, after fruitless struggles, his father died at Rodosto in Turkey, and was buried in Smyrna. The eldest son then received his father's Turkish pension, and was acknowledged Prince of Sie-benbürgen (Transylvania). He carried on the same warfare as his father, fought against and was driven away by Prince Ferdinand of Lob-kowitz, and finally died forgotten in Turkey. The younger brother took no part in the enterprises of his elder brother, and appears, therefore, to have been always on good terms with the Austrian Government."

Adverse writers have made much mystery over the fact that the Comte de St. Germain was rich and always had money at his disposal ; indeed, those writers who enjoyed calling him a " charlatan and a swindler " did not refrain also from hinting that his money must have been ill-gotten ; many even go so far as to say that he made it by deceiving people and exercising an undue influence over them. If we turn to the old *Archivarius* already mentioned, we find some very definite information that not only shows us whence the large fortune possessed by this mystic was derived, but also why he was so warmly welcomed by the King of France, and was so well known at all the courts of Europe. No obscure adventurer is this with whom we are dealing, but a man of princely blood, and of almost royal descent.

Turning back to the old chronicle we find in the volume for 1736 the will of the late Prince Franz-Leopold Ragoczy, in which both his sons are mentioned who have been already named, and also a third son.[1] It also states that Louis XIV. had bought landed property for this Prince Ragoczy from the Polish Queen Maria, the rents of which property were invested by the order of the King of France in the Hôtel de Ville in Paris. We also find that considerable legacies were left which were to be demanded from the Crown of France. The executors of this will were the Duc de Bourbon, the Duc de Maine and the Comte de Charleroi and Toulouse. To their care Prince Ragoczy committed his third son, to whom also he left a large legacy and other rights on this valuable property. Hence we must cast aside the theories that M. de St. Germain was a homeless and penniless adventurer, seeking to make money out of any kindly

---

[1] This is the son, mentioned by Prince Charles of Hesse, who was placed under the care of the last of the Medici.

disposed person. These were the views and ideas
of the newspaper and review writers of that day,
put forward in the leading periodicals. Unfortunately the law of heredity prevails in this class
of people, and there is a remarkable similarity
between the epithets hurled by the press of the
nineteenth century at the venturesome occultist
of to-day and those flung at M. de St. Germain
and other mystics of lesser importance and
minor merit.

We will now pass from this portion of our
subject to some of the personal incidents related
of M. de St. Germain ; perhaps the most interesting
are those given by one who knew him personally
in Anspach during the period that he was in
close connection with the Markgraf. It appears
that the mystic made two visits at different times
to Schwalbach, and thence he went to Triesdorf.
We will let the writer speak for himself on
this point :—

" On hearing that a stranger, both remarkable
and interesting, was at Schwalbach, the Markgraf
of Brandenburg-Anspach invited him to come
to Triesdorf in the spring, and the Graf Tzarogy
(for this was the name under which he appeared)
accepted this invitation, on the condition that
they would allow him to live in his own way
quite unnoticed and at peace.

He was lodged in the lower rooms of the

Castle, below those occupied by Mademoiselle
Clairon. The Markgraf and his wife lived in the
Falkenhaus. The Graf Tzarogy had no servant
of his own ; he dined as simply as possible in
his own room, which he seldom left. His wants
were extremely few, and he avoided all general
society, spending the evenings in the company
of only the Markgraf, Mademoiselle Clairon,
and those persons whom the former was pleased
to have around him. It was impossible to persuade the Graf Tzarogy to dine at the Prince's
table, and he only saw the Markgräfin a few
times, although she was very curious to make
the acquaintance of this strange individual. In
conversation the Graf was most entertaining,
and showed much knowledge of the world and
of men. He was always specially glad to speak
of his childhood and of his mother, to whom
he never referred without emotion, and often
with tears in his eyes. If one could believe
him, he had been brought up like a Prince.
One day Tzarogy showed the Markgraf an invitation which he had received, sent by a courier,
from the Graf Alexis Orloff, who was just
returning from Italy ; the letter pressed Graf
Tzarogy to pay him a visit, as Graf Orloff was
passing through Nuremberg. . . . The Markgraf
went with Graf Tzarogy to Nuremberg, where
the Graf Alexis Orloff had already arrived. On

their arrival Orloff, with open arms, came forward
to meet and embrace the Graf Tzarogy, who
now appeared for the first time in the uniform
of a Russian General ; and Orloff called him
several times, ' Caro padre,' ' Caro amico.'   The
Graf Alexis received the Markgraf of Brandenburg-Anspach with the most marked politeness,
and thanked him several times for the protection
which the Markgraf had accorded to his worthy
friend ;   they dined together at midday.   The
conversation was most interesting ;   they spoke
a good deal of the campaign in the Archipelago,
and still more about useful and scientific dis-
coveries.   Orloff showed the Markgraf a piece of
unignitable wood, which when tested produced
neither flames nor cinders, but simply fell to
pieces in light ashes, after it had swollen up
like a sponge.   After dinner Graf Orloff took
the Graf Tzarogy into the next room, where
they remained for some considerable time together.   The writer, who was standing at the
window under which the carriages of Graf
Orloff were drawn up, remarked that one of
the Graf's servants came, opened one of the
carriage doors and took out from the box under
the seat a large red leather bag, and carried it
upstairs to the other room.   After their return
to Anspach the Graf Tzarogy showed them,
for the first time, his credentials as a Russian

General with the Imperial seal attached; he afterwards informed the Markgraf that the name Tzarogy was an assumed name, and that his real name was Ragotzy, and that he was the sole representative and descendant of the late exiled Prince Ragotzy of Siebenbürgen of the time of the Emperor Leopold ".[1]

So far this narrative is tolerably accurate, but after this point the author proceeds with the history of what he considers the "unveiling" of the "notorious Comte de St. Germain," in which all the various theories about his birth, to which we have already referred, are retold with embellishments. Amongst other wild reports, it was stated that M. de St. Germain had only become acquainted with the Orloffs in Leghorn in 1770, whereas there are various historical proofs showing, without doubt, that he was in 1762 in St. Petersburg, where he knew the Orloffs well. We have moreover heard in Russia that he was staying with the Princess Marie Galitzin at Archangelskoï on March 3rd, 1762.

The following details were found in Russia, and sent by a Russian friend :—

" The Comte de St. Germain was here in the time of Peter III. and left when Catherine II.

---

[1] *Curiositäten der Literarisch-historischen Vor- und Mitwelt,* pp. 285, 286. Weimar, 1818.

came to the throne. M. Pyliaeff [1] thinks even before Catherine's time.

" At St. Petersburg St. Germain lived with Count Rotari, the famous Italian painter, who was the painter of the beautiful portraits which are in the Peterhof palace.

" The street where they lived is supposed to be the Grafsky péréoulok (' péréoulok ' means small street, and ' Grafsky' comes from Graf-Count) near the Anitchkoff bridge where the palace is, on the Newsky. St. Germain was a splendid violinist, he 'played like an orchestra.' In the ' Story of the Razoamovsky family' Alexis R. was reported to have spoken of a beautiful moonstone St. Germain had in his possession.

" M. Pyliaeff has seen (he cannot remember where now) a piece of music, some air for the harp, dedicated to Countess Ostermann by St. Germain's own hand *signed*. It is bound beautifully in red maroquin. The date is about 1760.

" M. Pyliaeff thinks that St. Germain was not in Moscow. He says the Youssoupoff family have many MSS. in old chests and that St. Germain was in relations with a Prince Youssoupoff to whom he gave the elixir for long life. He says, too, that St. Germain did not bear

[1] Told by M. Pyliaeff, member of the " Novoie Vremia," author of " Old Petersburg."

the name of Saltykoff (Soltikow) in Russia but that in Vienna he did take this name.

" About the music signed by St. Germain, M. Pyliaeff now recollects that it belonged to him himself. He bought it at some sale and had it for some time. Then he gave it to the famous composer Peter *Chaikowsky* as a present. It must now be in Chaikowsky's papers, but as the great musician had very little order, M. Pyliaeff thinks it very unlikely that it could be found, especially as at Chaikowsky's sudden death all was left without any directions being given about the property."

We have said that the political events in his family had to some extent shadowed the life of M. de St. Germain ; one remarkable instance of this we will now cite : it is, as far as we know, the only one in which he himself makes any direct reference to it, and it occurs some time later than the events which we have just been relating. After the return of the Markgraf from Italy, whither he had gone in 1776, and where he had heard some of the legends and fabrications above referred to, he appears to have sent the writer whom we have quoted to Schwalbach to see the Graf Tzarogy, and to test his *bona fides*. We will continue the history as he gives it. " On his arrival, he found M. de St. Germain ill in bed. When the matter was explained to him, he admitted with perfect coolness that he had assumed from time to time all the names mentioned, even down to that of Soltikow; but he said he was known on all sides, and to many people, under these names, as a man of honour, and that if any calumniator were venturing to accuse him of nefarious transactions, he was ready to exculpate himself in the most satisfactory manner, as soon as he knew of what he was accused, and who the accuser was who dared to attack him. He steadily asserted that he had not told the Markgraf any lies with reference to his name and his family. The proofs of his origin, however, were in the hands of a person on whom he was dependent (*i.e.*, the Emperor of Austria), a dependence which had brought on him, in the course of his life, the greatest *espionage.* . . . When he was asked why he had not informed the Markgraf about the different names under which he had appeared in so many different places, the Graf Tzarogy answered that he was under no obligations to the Markgraf, and that since he offended no one and did no person any harm, he would only give such personal information after and not before he had dealings with them. The Graf said he had never abused the confidence of the Markgraf; he had given his real name. . . . after this he still remained at Schwalbach." A little later the author of the paragraph just quoted remarks : " What resources M. de St. Germain had, to defray the necessary expenses of his existence, is hard to guess." [1]

It appears curious to us that the writer knew so little of contemporary history. As we have seen, all the sons of Prince Ragoczy were amply provided for, and the proofs were even more accessible than they are in our day. He goes on to say in conclusion : " It would be an ungrateful task to declare that this man was a swindler ; for this proofs are required and they are not to be had." This is truly an ingenious statement, but borders somewhat on libel ; to speak of any one as a swindler without any proof is beyond the bounds of ordinary fairness, and it is especially incongruous in view of the final paragraph, which is as follows : " As long as the Graf had dealings with the Markgraf, he never asked for anything, and never received anything of the slightest value, and never mixed himself up in anything which did not concern him. On account of his extremely simple life, his wants were very limited ; when he had money he shared it with the poor."

If we compare these words with those spoken of M. de St. Germain by his friend Prince Charles of Hesse, we shall find they are in perfect accord. The only wonder is that a writer

[1] *Curiositäten, op. cit.*, pp. 287, 289, 293, 294.

who speaks such words of praise can even hint that his subject might be a " swindler." If such words can be rightly spoken of an " adventurer," then would it be well for the world if a few more of like sort could be found.

We shall find similar extraordinary contradictions in various writers as we proceed further with the life of M. de St. Germain.

CHAPTER II

HIS TRAVELS AND KNOWLEDGE

THE pure cult of Nature in the earliest patriarchal days
. . . became the heirloom of those alone who could discern
the noumenon beneath the phenomenon. Later, the Initiates
transmitted their knowledge to the human kings, as their
divine Masters had passed it to their forefathers. It was
their prerogative and duty to reveal the secrets of Nature
that were useful to mankind. . . . No Initiate was one if he
could not heal—aye, recall to life from apparent death
(coma) those who, too long neglected, would have indeed
died during their lethargy. Those who showed such powers
were forthwith set above the crowds, and were regarded as
Kings and Initiates. *The Secret Doctrine*, iii. 263.

LET us now trace, as far as we can with any
detailed information, the steps of M. de St. Germain in some of his extended travels. That he had
been in Africa, India and China we gather from
various hints he gives us, and also from facts
stated by many writers at different times. That
such travels should seem aimless and trivial to
the same writers is not a matter of surprise,
but to students of mysticism, and especially
those to whom the " Great Lodge " is a fact
and a necessity in the spiritual evolution of
mankind, to those students the widely extended
travels of this " messenger " from that Lodge

will not be surprising; rather they will seek below the surface, and try to understand the mission and the work that he came to do among the children of men.

We must bear in mind, moreover, that in the ancient world the arts and sciences were regarded as divine gifts; the gifts of the gods. "Kings of the 'Divine Dynasties,' they gave the first impulse to civilization, and directed the mind with which they had endued men, to the invention and perfection of all the arts and sciences." [1]

Conceited in their shallow ignorance the generality of mankind scorn the gifts and turn away from the givers. Some few centuries ago such givers· and teachers were silenced at the stake, like Giordano Bruno, and many others whom time has now justified in the eyes of men. Then, later, after the reaction of free thought in the eighteenth century we find Mesmer and the Comte de St. Germain giving up, not their lives, but their good names and characters in trying to help those to whom they were sent by the Great Lodge.

Let us now take up the thread of these travels, and in order to make them as clear as possible follow them in the order of their dates.

These range, as we have seen in our last

[1] BLAVATSKY (H. P.). *The Secret Doctrine*, ii., p. 380. London, 1893.

chapter from 1710 to 1822. We shall, however, not be able to deal very fully with each period, for M. de St. Germain often disappeared for many months at a time. The earliest records we can gather are as follows :—

" There appeared at the Court [1] in these days an extraordinary man, who called himself Comte de St. Germain. At first he distinguished himself through his cleverness and the great diversity of his talents, but in another respect he soon aroused the greatest astonishment.

" The old Countess v. Georgy who fifty years earlier had accompanied her husband to Venice where he had the appointment of ambassador, lately met St. Germain at Mme. de Pompadour's. For some time she watched the stranger with signs of the greatest surprise, in which was mixed not a little fear. Finally, unable to control her excitement, she approached the Count more out of curiosity than in fear.

" ' Will you have the kindness to tell me,' said the Countess, ' whether your father was in Venice about the year 1710 ? '

" ' No, Madame,' replied the Count quite unconcerned, ' it is very much longer since I lost my father ; but I myself was living in Venice at the end of the last and the beginning of this century ; I had the honour to pay you court then,

[1] The Court of Louis XV.

and you were kind enough to admire a few
Barcarolles of my composing which we used to
sing together.'

"'Forgive me, but that is impossible; the Comte
de St. Germain I knew in those days was at least
45 years old, and you, at the outside, are that
age at present.'

"'Madame,' replied the Count smiling, 'I am
very old.'

"'But then you must be nearly 100 years old.'

"'That is not impossible.' And then the Count
recounted to Mme. v. Georgy a number of familiar
little details which had reference in common to
both, to their sojourn in the Venitian States. He
offered, if she still doubted him, to bring back
to her memory certain circumstances and remarks, which . . . .

"'No, no,' interrupted the old ambassadress,
'I am already convinced. For all that you are
a most extraordinary man, a devil.'

"'For pity's sake!' exclaimed St. Germain in
a thundering voice, 'no such names!'

"He appeared to be seized with a cramp-like
trembling in every limb, and left the room
immediately.

"I mean to get to know this peculiar man more
intimately.

"St. Germain is of medium height and elegant
manners; his features are regular; his complexion

brown ; his hair black ; his face mobile and full of genius ; his carriage bears the impress and the nobility common only to the great. The Count dresses simply but with taste. His only luxury consists of a large number of diamonds, with which he is fairly covered ; he wears them on every finger, and they are set in his snuffboxes and his watches. One evening he appeared at court with shoebuckles, which Herr v. Gontaut, an expert on precious stones, estimated at 200,000 Francs.

"A matter worthy of remark is that the Count speaks French, English, German, Italian, Spanish and Portuguese equally perfectly ; so much so that when he converses with any of the inhabitants of the above countries in their mother tongue, they are unable to discover the slightest foreign accent. The Learned and the Oriental scholars have proved the knowledge of the Count St. Germain. The former found him more apt in the languages of Homer and Virgil than themselves ; with the latter he spoke Sanscrit, Chinese, Arabic in such a manner as to show them that he had made some lengthy stay in Asia, and that the languages of the East were but poorly learned in the Colleges of Louis The Great and Montaigne.

"The Comte de St. Germain accompanied on the piano without music, not only every song but also the most difficult *concerti*, played on various instruments. Rameau was much impressed with the playing of this dilettante, and especially struck at his improvising.

" The Count paints beautifully in oils ; but that which makes his paintings so remarkable is a particular colour, a secret, which he has discovered, and which lends to the painting an extraordinary brilliancy. In his historical pieces, St. Germain always introduces into the dress of the women, sapphires, rubies and emeralds of such brilliant hue that they seem to have borrowed their beauty from the original gems. Vanloo, who never tires in his admiration of the surprising colouring, has often requested the Count to let him participate in his secret ; the latter, however, will not divulge it.

" Without attempting to sit in judgement on the knowledge of a fellow-being, of whom at this very moment that I am writing, both court and town have exhausted all surmises, one can, I think, well assert that a portion of his miracles is due to his knowledge of physics and chemistry in which sciences he is well grounded. At all events it is palpable that his knowledge has laid the seeds for him of sound good health ; a life which will — or which has overstepped the ordinary time allotted to man ; and has also endowed him with the means of preventing the ravages of time from affecting the body. Among other statements, concerning the Count's astounding qualities, made to the Favourite by Mme. v. Georgy after her first meeting with the Count after this lapse of years, was that during her first stay in Venice, she received from him an Elixir which for fully a quarter of a century preserved unaltered the youthful charms she possessed at 25. Elderly gentlemen, whom Mme. de Pompadour questioned concerning this peculiar incident, gave the assurance that this was the truth, adding that the standing still in youthful appearance of Mme. v. Georgy supported by the testimony of these old men would make it appear still more probable.

"One evening at a party St. Germain accompanied several Italian airs for the young Comtesse afterwards so celebrated under the name of Comtesse de Genlis, then aged ten years.

"When she had finished singing, the Count said to her : ' in five or six years you will have a very beautiful voice, which you will preserve a long time ; in order to perfect the charm you should also preserve your beauty ; this will be your happy fate between your 16th and 17th year.'

"'But, Count,' answered the child, while allowing her pretty fingers to glide over the notes, ' that does not lie in any one's power.'

"'Oh yes,' answered the Count carelessly,

' only tell me whether it would give you pleasure to remain at that age ? '

" ' Truly that would be charming.'

" ' Well I promise it you.' And St. Germain spoke of other matters.

" Encouraged by the friendliness of this fashionable man, the Countess' mother ventured to ask him if Germany was his Fatherland.

" ' Madame,' said he, sighing deeply, ' there are some things of which one may not speak. Suffice it to know that at seven years of age I was wandering in woods, and that a price was set upon my head. On my birthday my mother, whom I was not to see again, bound her portrait round my arm ; I will shew it to you.'

" At these words St. Germain threw up his sleeve and shewed the ladies the miniature of an exceptionally beautiful woman, but represented in rather a peculiar costume.

" ' To what date does this dress belong ? ' asked the young Countess. Without answering this question, the Count put down his sleeve again, and brought forward another topic. Every day one was surprised by a fresh miracle in Count St. Germain's company. Some little time previously he had brought Mme. de Pompadour a *bonbonnière* which was universally admired. It was worked very beautifully in black enamel, and on the lid was an agate. The Count begged the Marquise to place the *bonbonnière* near the fire ; a few minutes later she went to take it away. How great was the astonishment of all present : the agate had disappeared, and in its place was to be seen a pretty shepherdess in the midst of her flock.

"After the *bonbonnière* had again been placed near the fire, the shepherdess disappeared, and the agate re-appeared." [1]

This episode was written down in 1750, but the facts mentioned took place in 1723. It must be carefully noticed that all the personal friends of M. de St. Germain were in high position, chiefly Austrians and Hungarians, all men of high birth and noble family, his own kith and kin ; among them we find Prince Kaunitz, Prince Ferdinand Lobkowitz, Graf Zobor, Graf Maximilian Joseph von Lamberg, men of public position, and well known families.

From 1737 to 1742, our mystic was at the Court of the Shah of Persia, and it is here that he probably acquired his knowledge of diamonds and precious stones, for according to his own very credible statement, it was here that he began to understand the secrets of Nature ; but his arduously acquired knowledge leads us to infer a long period of careful study. These hints

[1] Taken from "*Chroniques de l'Œil de Bœuf*." Written down by the widowed Countess v. B. . . .

we gather from F. W. von Barthold [1] in his interesting work, and they confirm the statement made by another writer that M. de St. Germain had been pursuing his researches in Persia.

We next find him in England, during the Jacobite Revolution of 1745, suspected as a spy, and arrested. Two interesting extracts can here be quoted.

The first is from Horace Walpole's [2] amusing letters to Sir Horace Mann, the British Envoy at Florence. Writing on Dec. 9th, 1745, Walpole, after relating all the excitements produced by the Revolution, says : " The other day they seized an odd man who goes by the name of Count St. Germain. He has been here these two years, and will not tell who he is or whence, but professes that he does not go by his right name. He sings and plays on the violin wonderfully, is mad, and not very sensible."

The second reference to this stay in England may be found in Read's *Weekly Journal or British Gazetteer*, May 17th, 1760, and is as follows :

" The author of the Brussels' Gazette tells us that the person who styles himself Comte de St. Germain, who lately arrived here from Hol-

[1] BARTHOLD (F. W. von), *Die Geschichtlichen Persönlichkeiten in Jacob Casanova's Mémoiren*, Vol. ii., Berlin 1846.
[2] *Letters of Horace Walpole, Earl of Orford, to Sir Horace Mann*, ii., pp. 108, 109. London, 1833.

land, was born in Italy in 1712. He speaks
German and French as fluently as Italian, and
expresses himself pretty well in English. He
has a smattering of all the arts and sciences, is
a good chemist, a virtuoso in musick, and a very
agreeable companion. In 1746 [1745 according
to Walpole], he was on the point of being ruined
in England. One who was jealous of him with
a lady, slipt a letter into his pocket as from
the young Pretender (thanking him for his services and desiring him to continue them), and
immediately had him taken up by a messenger.
His innocence being fully proved on his examination, he was discharged out of the custody
of the messenger and asked to dinner by Lord H.
[Probably William Stanhope, Earl of Harrington,
who was Secretary of the Treasury and Treasurer
of the Chamber at this date ; he died 1760.]
Those who know him will be sorry (says M.
Maubert) to hear that he has incurred the Christian
king's displeasure."

This last paragraph alludes to what occurred
at a later period.

After this date, 1745, it seems that M. de St.
Germain went to Vienna, and spent some time,
in that city,[1] and in 1755 went to India, for

---

[1] " He had lived as a prince in Vienna from 1745 to 1746,
was very well received, and the first minister of the Emperor
[Francis I.], Prince Ferdinand von Lobkowitz, was his most

the second time, as we gather from a letter of his written to the Graf von Lamberg, to which we shall refer again later on.

" I am indebted," he writes, " for my knowledge of melting jewels to my second journey to India, in the year 1755, with General Clive, who was under Vice Admiral Watson. On my first journey I had only a very faint idea of the wonderful secret of which we are speaking ; all the attempts that I made in Vienna, Paris and London, are worthless as experiments ; the great work was interrupted at the time I have mentioned."

Every writer, adverse or favourable, mentions and lays stress on the wonderful power of improving precious stones that was possessed by M. de St. Germain. Indeed almost every sort of art seems to have been more or less known to him, judging by the many testimonies that we have on these points.

Our next date, 1757, brings us to the period which is best known to the public. M. de St. Germain was introduced at Paris by the then Minister of War, Maréchal and Comte de Belle-

intimate friend. The latter introduced him to the French Maréchal de Belle-Isle who had been sent by King Louis XV. on a special embassy to the Court at Vienna. Belle-Isle, the wealthy grandson of Fouquet, was so taken with the brilliant and witty St. Germain, that he persuaded him to accompany him on a visit to Paris." *Historische Herinneringen*, van C. A. van SYPESTEYN ; 'sGravenhage, 1869.

Isle ; but as we have seen from the records already cited, neither M. de St. Germain nor his family were unknown to Louis XV. Hence we do not wonder at the cordial and gracious reception with which he met, nor can we be astonished that the king assigned him a suite of rooms at his royal Château of Chambord. Here there was a laboratory fitted up for experiments, and a group of students gathered round our mystic. Among these we find the Baron de Gleichen, and Marquise d'Urfé and also the Princess of Anhalt-Zerbst, mother of Catherine II. of Russia. Madame de Genlis,[1] speaking of him at this period, says :—

" He was well acquainted with physics, and was a very great chemist. My father, who was well qualified to judge, was a great admirer of his abilities in this way. . . . He had discovered a secret respecting colours which was really wonderful, and which gave an extraordinary effect to his pictures. . . . M. de St. Germain never would consent to give up his secret." Madame du Hausset relates in her memoirs an interesting instance of his knowledge of precious stones.

" The King," says she, " ordered a middling-sized diamond which had a flaw in it, to be

[1] GENLIS (Comtesse de), *Mémoires Inédits pour servir à l'Histoire des XVIII. et XIX. Siècles*, p. 88. Paris, 1825.

brought to him. After having it weighed, his
Majesty said to the Comte : ' The value of this
diamond as it is, and with the flaw in it, is six
thousand livres ; without the flaw it would be
worth at least ten thousand. Will you undertake
to make me a gainer of four thousand livres ? '
St. Germain examined it very attentively, and
said, ' It is possible ; it may be done. I will
bring it to you again in a month.'

"At the time appointed the Comte de St.
Germain brought back the diamond without a
spot, and gave it to the King. It was wrapped
in a cloth of amianthos, which he took off. The
king had it weighed immediately, and found it
very little diminished. His Majesty then sent
it to his jeweller by M. de Gontaut, without
telling him of anything that had passed. The
jeweller gave him nine thousand six hundred
livres for it. The King, however, sent for the
diamond back again, and said he would keep
it as a curiosity. He could not overcome his surprise, and said M. de St. Germain must be
worth millions, especially if he possessed the
secret of making large diamonds out of small
ones. The Comte neither said that he could or
could not, but positively asserted that he knew
how to make pearls grow, and give them the
finest water. The King paid him great attention,
and so did Madame de Pompadour. M. du Ques-

noy once said that St. Germain was a quack, but the King reprimanded him. In fact, his Majesty appears infatuated with him, and sometimes talks of him as if his descent were illustrious."

One fact in this Parisian period must not be omitted ; it appears from statements made by Madame du Hausset,[1] Herr von Barthold and the Baron de Gleichen, that a young Englishman, at that time resident in Paris, Lord Gower by name, used to amuse himself and other idle people by passing himself off as M. de St. Germain, so that most of the silly and foolish tales about him, which ran riot in the gossiping " salons " of the period, originated in the sayings of this idle young fellow. Various details of his doings are to be found, but they are not worth further notice, beyond the fact that M. de St. Germain had to bear the blame for utterances which did not originate with him. Says Heer van Sypesteyn :[2] "Many of the wild stories had probably nothing to do with M. de St. Germain and were invented with the object of injuring him and making him ridiculous. A certain Parisian wag, known as ' Milord Gower,' was a splendid mimic, and went into Paris salons to

[1] HAUSSET (Madame du), *Mémoires*, p. 148, seq. ; Paris, 1824.
[2] *Op. cit.*

play the part of St. Germain—naturally it was very exaggerated, but very many people were taken in by this make-believe St. Germain.

Meanwhile our philosopher worked on with those whom he was able to help and teach in various ways. In 1760 we find him sent by Louis XV. to the Hague on a political mission : the circumstances are variously told by different writers. In April, 1760, we find M. de St. Germain passing through East Friesland to England.[1] Next, in *The London Chronicle* of June 3rd, 1760, we have a long account of a " mysterious foreigner," who had just arrived on England's shores. It is also said by one writer that he was well received at Court, and many papers of the period mention him as a " person of note " to whom marked attention was paid.[2]

[1] HEZEKIEL i. *op. cit.*

[2] *Gazette of the Netherlands.* Jan. 12th, 1761.

The Hague, Jan. 2nd.

" Letters from Paris state that when starting for this country, to which he came without asking permission of the King, M. de St. Germain returned his Red Ribbon : but it is practically certain that he has an understanding with the King of Denmark.

" The 3rd.

" The so-called Count of St. Germain is an incomprehensible man of whom nothing is known : neither his name nor his origin, nor his position ; he has an income, no one knows from whence it is derived ; acquaintances, no one knows where he made them ; entry into the Cabinets of Princes without being acknowledged by them ! "

In the British Museum there are pieces of music composed by the Comte de St. Germain on both his visits, for they are dated 1745 and 1760. It was said everywhere, by enemies as well as by friends, that he was a splendid violinist ; he " played like an orchestra."

There is one most interesting souvenir of M. de St. Germain, which we have had the good fortune to see. It is preserved in the library of the grand old castle of Raudnitz in Bohemia, the property of Prince Ferdinand von Lobkowitz.

Amongst the MSS. and other treasures of that rare collection we found a book of music composed by M. de St. Germain, from which, by the gracious permission of the present Prince, we have had traced the inscription and autograph. It runs thus :—

" Pour le Prince de Lobkowitz, Musique Raisonée, selon le bon sens, aux Dames Angloises qui aiment le vrai goût en cet art.

" Par . . . de St. Germain."

The first letter, or letters, of the signature are quite undecipherable, although they have been most carefully traced for us by the librarian at Raudnitz.

We next have to pass on to St. Petersburg where, according to the words of the Graf Gregor Orloff to the Margrave of Brandenburg-

Anspach, M. de St. Germain had "played a great part in their revolution." [1]

He is mentioned as having been in St. Petersburg by another writer, or rather in an anonymous book, the translation of the title of which runs :

" A few Words about the First Helpers of Catherine II." (xviii. Bk. 3, p. 343, 1869).

The writer has other details in her possession, but as they are at present unverified and come rather as fragments, it is better to wait for more accurate information, which she hopes to procure. Various hints, however, lead us to suppose that M. de St. Germain passed some time in Russia. As we have noticed already the Princess of Anhalt-Zerbst, the mother of Catherine II., was very friendly to him ; indeed he passed much time at her house in Paris.

In 1763, however, we get a deeply interesting account of our philosopher in the shape of a letter from the Graf Karl Cobenzl to the Prince Kaunitz, the Prime Minister. The details it gives are so interesting that it is better to quote it in full :—

" BRUSSELS, *April 8th*, 1763.

" GRAF KARL COBENZL TO KAUNITZ.

" It was about three months ago that the

---

[1] *Curiositäten der Literarisch-historischen Vor und Mitwelt,* pp. 285, 286. Weimar, 1818.

Raudnitz on the Elbe in Bohemia, the property of Prince Ferdinand von Lobkovitz.

person known by the name of the Comte de St. Germain passed this way, and came to see me. I found him the most singular man that I ever saw in my life. I do not yet precisely know his birth ; I believe, however, that he is the son of a clandestine union in a powerful and illustrious family. Possessing great wealth, he lives in the greatest simplicity ; he knows everything, and shows an uprightness, a goodness of soul, worthy of admiration. Among a number of his accomplishments, he made, under my own eyes, some experiments, of which the most important were the transmutation of iron into a metal as beautiful as gold, and at least as good for all goldsmith's work ; the dyeing and preparation of skins, carried to a perfection which surpassed all the moroccos in the world, and the most perfect tanning ; the dyeing of silks, carried to a perfection hitherto unknown ; the like dyeing of woollens ; the dyeing of wood in the most brilliant colours penetrating through and through, and the whole without either indigo or cochineal, with the commonest ingredients, and consequently at a very moderate price ; the composition of colours for painting, ultra-marine is as perfect as is made from lapis lazuli ; and finally, removing the smell from painting oils, and making the best oil of Provence from the oils of Navette, of Colsat, and from others, even

the worst. I have in my hands all these productions, made under my own eyes ; I have had
them undergo the most strict examinations, and
seeing in these articles a profit which might
mount up to millions, I have endeavoured to
take advantage of the friendship that this man
has felt for me, and to learn from him all these
secrets. He has given them to me, and he asks
nothing for himself beyond a payment proportionate to the profits that may accrue from them,
it being understood that this shall be only when
the profit has been made. As the marvellous
must inevitably seem uncertain, I have avoided
the two points which appeared to me to be
feared, the first, the being a dupe, and the
second, the involving myself in too great an
expenditure. To avoid the first, I took a trusty
person, under whose eyes I had the experiments
made, and I was fully convinced of the reality
and the cheapness of these productions. And as
to the second, I referred M. de Zurmont (which
is the name that St. Germain has taken) to a
good and trustworthy merchant at Tournay, with
whom he is working, and I have had advances
made which mount up to very little, through
Nettine, whose son, and the son-in-law of Wal-
ckiers, are the persons who will carry on these
manufactures, when the profits of the first
experiments place us in a position to establish

House at Amsterdam where the Comte de St. Germain lived in 1762.

them, without risking anything of our own. The moment for deriving the profit is already close at hand ".[1]

From another source, also, we hear of de St. Germain at Tournay, namely, from the memoirs of Casanova.

" Casanova on the road to Tournay was informed of the presence of M. le Comte de St. Germain, and desired to be presented to him. Being told that the Comte received no one, he wrote him to request an interview, which was granted under the restriction of coming *incognito*, and not being invited to partake of food with him. Casanova found the Comte in the dress of an Armenian with a long beard."

In this interview, M. de St. Germain informed Casanova that he was arranging a *Fabrique* for the Graf Cobenzl [2].

From 1763, the date at which we have now arrived, up to 1769, we only get the details of one year in Berlin, and this account comes from the memoirs of M. Dieudonné Thiébault, who gives the following interesting sketch :

" There came to Berlin and remained in that city for the space of a year a remarkable man, who passed by the name of the Comte de St.

---

[1] ARNETH (A. Ritter von), *Graf Philipp Cobenzl und seine Mémoiren*, p. 9, note. Wien, 1885.
[2] CASANOVA (F. Seingalt de), *Mémoires :* vi., p. 76.

Germain. The Abbé Pernety was not slow in recognising in him the characteristics which go to make up an adept, and came to us with wonderful stories."

The author then goes on to relate that the Princess Amélie went to call on him, and he also remarks that the old Baron Knyhausen was always addressed by M. de St. Germain as " my son." Says our author :—

" Madame de Troussel was also anxious to see him. The Abbé Pernety arranged the matter for her, and the Comte came to her house one evening to supper. They chanced to make mention of the ' Philosopher's Stone,' and the Comte curtly observed that most people who were in pursuit of that were astonishingly illogical, inasmuch as they employed no agent but fire, forgetting that fire breaks up and decomposes, and that consequently it was mere folly to depend upon it for the building up of a new composition. He dwelt much upon this, and finally led the conversation back to more general topics. In appearance M. de St. Germain was refined and intellectual. He was clearly of gentle birth, and had moved in good society ; and it was reported that the famous Cagliostro (so well known for his mystification of Cardinal Rohan and others at Paris) had been his pupil. The pupil, however, never reached the level of his

master and, while the latter finished his career
without mishap, Cagliostro was often rash to the
point of criminality, and died in the prison of
the Inquisition at Rome. . . . In the history of
M. de St. Germain, we have the history of a wise
and prudent man who never wilfully offended
against the code of honour, or did aught that
might offend our sense of probity. Marvels
we have without end, never anything mean or
scandalous." [1]

The exact date of this visit to Berlin we cannot
accurately give, but it comes in before the stay
in Venice, where he was found by the Graf Max
von Lamberg,[2] at this time Chamberlain to the
Emperor Joseph II., and in his book we have some
most interesting details. The Graf finds M. de
St. Germain under the name of Marquis d'Aymar,
or Belmare, making a variety of experiments
with flax, which he was bleaching to look like
Italian silk ; he had established quite a large
place, and had about a hundred workers. It
would appear that he then travelled with the
Graf von Lamberg, for in a paper published at
Florence *Le notizie del Mondo* (July, 1770), under
the heading " News of the World," we find the
following paragraph :—

[1] THIÉBAULT (D.), *Mes Souvenirs de Vingt Ans de Séjour
à Berlin*, iv., p. 83. Paris, 1813.
[2] LAMBERG (Graf Max von), *Le Mémorial d'un Mondain*,
p 80. London, 1775.

" TUNIS, *July* 1770.

" The Comte Maximilian de Lamberg,[1] Chamberlain of M.M.L.L. II. and RR. having paid a visit to the Island of Corsica to make various investigations, has been staying here since the end of June, in company with the Signor de St. Germain, celebrated in Europe for the vastness of his political and philosophical knowledge."

No further details are given of this journey, but we hear of M. de St. Germain being in Mantua in the year 1773.

One important point which belongs to the year 1770 has been omitted. M. de St. Germain was at Leghorn when the Russian fleet was there ; he wore a Russian uniform, and was called Graf Saltikoff by the Graf Alexis Orloff. It was, moreover, in this year that he returned to Paris, on the disgrace of the Prime Minister, his enemy, the Duc de Choiseul.

" All his abilities, especially his extraordinary kindness," says Heer van Sypesteyn (*op. cit.*), " yes, even magnanimity, which formed his essential characteristics, had made him so re-

[1] Some interesting matter concerning the Comte de St. Germain is printed in a most interesting book lately published, *Casanova et son temps*, by E. Maynial. One entirely new and most ꞌinteresting fact is given by him : a correspondence has been found at Prague between the Comte de Lamberg and M. de St. Germain and is now in the hands of a well known Austrian writer, who is putting it in order ; no doubt before long M. Gugitz will publish these documents.

spected and so beloved, that when in 1770, after
the fall of the Duc de Choiseul, his arch enemy,
he again appeared in Paris, it was only with the
greatest expressions of sorrow that the Parisians
allowed him to depart. . . . M. de St. Germain
came to the Hague after the death of Louis XV.
(May 10th, 1774), and left for Schwalbach in
1774. This was the last time he visited Holland.
It cannot be ascertained with accuracy how often
he was there. . . . It is stated in a German
biography that he was in Holland in 1710, 1735,
1742, 1748, 1760 and 1773."

This last date brings us to the period that we
have already noticed, the stay at Triesdorf and
at Schwalbach, where many alchemical and other
experiments were carried on by the Markgraf
and the Comte. The former we hear was proud
of his medical knowledge, and obtained from the
English Consul at Leghorn a copy of the pre-
scription for the " Russian Tea " or " Aqua
Benedetta," made by M. de St. Germain, which
was used in the Russian fleet, then in the Archipelago, to preserve the health of the troops under
the severe heat.

From 1774 until 1776 we have the visit to
Triesdorf; in 1776 we hear of our mystic in Leipzig, and the following year in Dresden ; with these
periods we shall have to deal in our next paper.
About 1779 we hear of M. de St. Germain at

Hamburg ; thence he goes to Prince Karl of Hesse and stays with him for some time as his loved and honoured guest. They began various experiments together, experiments which were in all cases to be of use to the human race. Writing of the knowledge and alluding to the early education of M. de St. Germain by the Duc de Medici, the Prince says :

" This House (Medici), as is well known, was in possession of the highest knowledge, and it is not surprising that he should have drawn his earlier knowledge from them ; but he claimed to have learned that of Nature by his own application and researches. He thoroughly understood herbs and plants, and had invented the medicines of which he constantly made use, and which prolonged his life and health. I still have all his recipes, but the physicians ran riot much against his science after his death. There was a physician, Lossau, who had been an apothecary, and to whom I gave 1,200 crowns a year to work at the medicines which the Comte de St. Germain taught him, among others and chiefly his tea, which the rich bought and the poor received gratis. . . . After the death of this physician, disgusted by the talk I heard on all sides, I withdrew all the recipes, and I did not replace Lossau." [1]

[1] HESSE-CASSEL, *op. cit.*, p. 135.

Looking back at the record of all the powers and abilities possessed by this great man, one point comes out clearly : either he was following some definite plan, a plan not known to the general world, or he wandered from place to place without aim, without family, without human ties—a sorrowful life, truly, for so gifted a mortal, if this were so. But since he appeared always contented, though knowing more than those with whom he came into contact, always giving, and never in need, ever helping, but never claiming aid—surely with such evidence it becomes obvious to even the critical sceptic that some power, some plan, must have guided the footsteps and life of the Comte de St. Germain. Indeed, one of the writers before quoted says :

" Sometimes he fell into a trance, and when he again recovered, he said he had passed the time while he lay unconscious in far-off lands ; sometimes he disappeared for a considerable time, then suddenly re-appeared, and let it be understood that he had been in another world in communication with the dead. Moreover, he prided himself on being able to tame bees, and to make snakes listen to music." [1]

The author seems unaware that the ordinary Yogis of India have this power over snakes ; and doubtless M. de St. Germain learned his

[1] SYPESTEYN (J. van) *Historische Herinneringen.*

knowledge in India. The power, also, of communicating with the dead has had more light thrown on it in this nineteenth century, thanks to those who follow in the footsteps of M. de St. Germain and who are aiding in the same great work. Nevertheless, although the above-quoted writer is sceptical on these points, he awards a tribute of honest merit to our philosopher worth noticing, when writing :—

" However this may be, St. Germain was in many respects a remarkable man, and wherever he was personally known he left a favourable impression behind, and the remembrance of many good and sometimes of many noble deeds. Many a poor father of a family, many a charitable institution, was helped by him in secret . . . not one bad, nor one dishonourable action was ever known of him, and so he inspired sympathy everywhere, and not least in Holland."

Thus clearly stands out the character of one who by some is called a " messenger " from that spiritual Hierarchy by whom the world's evolution is guided ; such is the moral worth of the man whom the shallow critics of the earth call " adventurer."

CHAPTER III

THE COMING DANGER

THE following extracts are translated from the
very rare and valuable *Souvenirs de Marie-
Antoinette*, by the Countess d'Adhémar, who had
been an intimate friend of the Queen, and who
died in 1822.

I have not been able to find a single copy of
this rare work [1] in any library in England, or on
the Continent, to which I have so far had access.
But fortunately a copy exists at Odessa in the
library of Madame Fadéef, the aunt and friend
of Madame H. P. Blavatsky, and this may lend
it an additional interest in the opinion of some of
our readers.

One of our members has been kindly permitted
to make some extracts from the four volumes,

---

[1] Since this was written I have been able to get this work ;
and the present Comtesse d'Adhémar informed me that
there are documents concerning the Comte de St. Germain in
their family papers.

Madame H. P. Blavatsky was visiting the family and stayed
at the Château d'Adhémar in 1884. This was one of the
numerous aristocratic families which were ruined in the
Revolution. The present Comtesse d'Adhémar is an American ; the documents are in America.

and thanks are due to Madame Fadéef for so graciously lending the work for this purpose. Madame d'Adhémar appears to have kept a daily diary, after the fashion of the period, and to have later written her *Souvenirs* from this diary, occasionally interjecting an explanatory remark. They cover a long period of time, ranging from 1760 to 1821.

One very interesting fact as to dates occurs in a note written by the hand of the Countess, fastened with a pin to the original MS. and dated May 12th, 1821. She died in 1822. It refers to a prophecy made to her by St. Germain about the year 1793, when he warned her of the approaching sad fate of the Queen, and in response to her query as to whether she would see him again, he replied, " Five times more ; do not wish for the sixth."

The Countess writes : " I saw M. de St. Germain again, and always to my unspeakable surprise : at the assassination of the Queen ; at the coming of the 18th Brumaire ; the day following the death of the Duke d'Enghien [1804] ; in the month of January, 1813 ; and on the eve of the murder of the Duke de Berri [1820]. I await the sixth visit when God wills."

These dates are of interest because of the generally received opinion that St. Germain died in 1784 ; some few writers say he only retired from public work. These varying opinions will be treated later.

Says Madame d'Adhémar [1] :—

" Since my pen is again writing the name of the Comte de St. Germain, I will say something about him. He appeared (that is the word) at the Court of France long before me. It was in 1743 ; the rumour spread that a stranger, enormously rich to judge by the magnificence of his jewellery, had just arrived at Versailles. Whence did he come ? That is what no one has ever been able to learn. His countenance, haughty, intellectual, acute, struck one at first sight. He had a pliant, graceful figure, delicate hands, a small foot, an elegant leg which set off a well-fitting silk stocking. The small-clothes, very tight, also suggested a rare perfection of form ; his smile showed the most beautiful teeth in the world, a pretty dimple adorned his chin, his hair was black, his eyes were soft and penetrating. Oh ! what eyes ! I have nowhere seen their equal. He appeared about forty to forty-five years old. He was met again in the smaller apartments where he had free admission, at the beginning of 1768. He did not see Madame du Barry, but he was present at the catastrophe of Madame de Chateauroux.

" When this lady died, the King who had only

[1] ADHÉMAR, *op. cit.*, vol. I, p. 294.

known the Count for a year, had nevertheless so much confidence in him that he asked him for an antidote for the dying Duchess. The Count refused, saying : ' It is too late.' " She continues : " At this same period a very singular adventure befell me. I was alone in Paris, M. d'Adhémar having gone to visit some relations of his own name that he had in Languedoc. It was one Sunday at eight o'clock in the morning. I am accustomed to hear Mass at noon, so that I had but little time for my toilette and for preparing to go out. I rose hurriedly, then, and had scarcely thrown on my morning wrapper when Mdlle. Rostande, my head waiting-woman in whom also I placed entire confidence, came in to tell me that a gentleman wished to speak to me.

" To pay a visit to a woman at eight o'clock was against all accepted rules. ' Is it my procurator, my lawyer ? ' I asked. For one has always one of these gentlemen at one's heels, however little property one may possess. ' Is it my architect, my saddler, or one of my farmers ? '

" To each question a negative answer.

" ' But who is it, then, my dear ? '

" I treated my maid with familiarity. She was born the same day as myself, in the same house, that of my father, with the difference that I came into the world in a handsome apartment and she in the lodge of our house porter. Her father, a worthy Languedoc man, was a super-annuated pensioner in our service.

" ' I thought,' answered my maid, ' with all due respect to Madame la Comtesse, that the devil had long since made a mantle out of the skin of this personage.'

" I passed in review all those of my acquaintance who could have deserved any special treatment by Satan, and I found so many of them that I did not know on whom to fasten my conjectures.

" ' Since Madame does not guess,' continued Mdlle. Rostande, ' I will take the liberty of telling her that it is the Comte de Saint-Germain ! '

" ' Comte de Saint-Germain ! ' I exclaimed, ' the man of miracles.'

" ' Himself.'

" My surprise was great on finding that he was at Paris and in my house. It was eight years since he had left France, and no one knew in the least what had become of him. Heeding nothing but my curiosity, I ordered her to show him in.

" ' Did he tell you to announce him to me under his own name ? '

" ' It is M. de Saint-Noël that he calls himself now. No matter, I should recognise him among a thousand.'

" She went out, and a moment after the Count appeared. He looked fresh and well, and almost grown younger. He paid me the same compliment, but it may be doubted whether it was as sincere as mine.

" ' You have lost,' I said to him, ' a friend, a protector in the late King.'

" ' I doubly regret this loss, both for myself and for France.'

" ' The nation is not of your opinion ; it looks to the new reign for its welfare.'

" ' It is a mistake ; this reign will be fatal to it.'

" ' What are you saying ? ' I replied, lowering my voice and looking around me.

" ' The truth. . . . A gigantic conspiracy is being formed, which as yet has no visible chief, but he will appear before long. The aim is nothing less than the overthrow of what exists, to reconstruct it on a new plan. There is ill-will towards the royal family, the clergy, the nobility, the magistracy. There is still time, however, to baffle the plot ; later, this would be impossible.'

" ' Where have you seen all this ? Is it in dreaming, or awake ? '

" ' Partly with the help of my two ears, and partly through revelations. The King of France, I repeat, has no time to lose.'

" ' You must seek an audience of the Comte de

Maurepas, and let him know your fears, for he can do everything, being entirely in the confidence of the King.'

" 'He can do everything I know, except save France ; or rather, it is he who will hasten her ruin. This man will undo you, Madame.'

" 'You are telling me enough about it to get yourself sent to the Bastille for the rest of your days.'

" 'I do not speak thus except to friends of whom I am sure.'

" 'Nevertheless, see M. de Maurepas ; he has good intentions, though wanting in ability.'

" 'He would reject the evidence ; besides, he detests me. Do you not know the silly quatrain which caused his exile ?

> ' Beautiful Marquise, they praise your charms.
> Lovely are you and very frank ;
> But all that does not prevent
> Your flowers being flowers.'

" 'The rhyme is inaccurate, Count.'

" 'Oh ! the Marquise paid little attention to it ; but she knew that M. de Maurepas was the author of it, and he pretended that I had taken away the original manuscript from him to send it to the haughty Sultana. His exile followed the publication of these wretched verses, and from that time he included me in his schemes of vengeance. He will never forgive me. Neverthless, Madame

la Comtesse, this is what I propose to you.
Speak of me to the Queen, of the services that I
have rendered to the government in the missions
that have been entrusted to me at the various
courts of Europe. If her Majesty will listen to
me, I will reveal to her what I know ; then she
will judge whether it will be well for me to enter
into the King's presence ; without the inter-
vention, however, of M. de Maurepas—that is my
sine quâ non.'

" I listened attentively to M. de Saint-Germain,
and I understood all the dangers that would
again fall on my head, if I interfered in such an
affair. On the other hand, I knew the Count to
be perfectly conversant with European politics,
and I feared to lose the opportunity of serving
the State and the King. The Comte de Saint-
Germain, guessing my perplexity, said to me :—

" ' Think over my proposal ; I am in Paris
incognito ; do not speak of me to anyone ; and if
to-morrow you will come to meet me in the
church of the Jacobins in the Rue Saint-Honoré,
I will await your answer there at eleven o'clock
precisely.'

" ' I would rather see you in my own house.'

" ' Willingly ; to-morrow, then, Madame.'

" He departed. I pondered all day on this
apparition, as it were, and on the menacing words
of the Comte de Saint-Germain. What ! we were

on the eve of social disorganisation ; this reign, which was ushered in under such happy auspices, was brewing the tempest ! After long meditation on this text, I determined to present M. de Saint-Germain to the Queen, if she consented to it. He was punctual to the appointment, and delighted at the resolution that I had made. I asked him if he was going to settle in Paris ; he answered in the negative, his plans no longer permitting him to live in France.

" ' A century will pass,' he said, ' before I shall re-appear there.'

" I burst out laughing, and he did the same. That very day I went to Versailles ; I passed through the small apartments, and finding Madame de Misery there, I begged her to let the Queen know that I wished to see her as soon as she could receive me. The head chamber-woman returned with the command to conduct me in. I entered ; the Queen was sitting in front of a charming porcelain writing-table, which the King had given her ; she was writing, and turning her head she said to me with one of her gracious smiles :—

" ' What do you want with me ? '

" ' A trifle, Madame ; I merely aspire to save the monarchy.'

" Her Majesty looked at me with amazement.

" ' Explain yourself.'

"At this command I mentioned the Comte de Saint-Germain ; I told all that I knew of him, of his intimacy with the late King, Madame de Pompadour, the Duke de Choiseul ; I spoke of the real services that he had rendered to the State by his diplomatic ability ; I added that since the death of the Marquise he had disappeared from Court, and that no one knew the place of his retirement. When I had sufficiently piqued the Queen's curiosity, I ended by repeating to her what the Count had said to me the previous day, and had confirmed that morning.

"The Queen appeared to reflect ; then she replied.

"'It is strange ; yesterday I received a letter from my mysterious correspondent ; he warned me that an important communication would shortly be made to me, and that I must take it into serious consideration, on pain of the greatest misfortunes. The coincidence of these two things is remarkable, unless, however, they come from the same source ; what do you think about it ? '

"'I scarcely know what to say of it. Here has the Queen been receiving these mysterious communications for several years, and the Comte de Saint-Germain re-appeared only yesterday.'

"'Perhaps he acts in this way in order the better to conceal himself.'

"'That is possible ; nevertheless, something tells me that one ought to put faith in his words.'

I'll suck your dick.
If you suck mine

☐ Yes

☐ No

Only if I can stick it
in your Sisters ass, first.

" ' After all, one is not sorry to see him, were it only in passing. I authorise you, then, to bring him to-morrow to Versailles, disguised in your livery. He shall remain in your apartments, and as soon as it is possible for me to admit him, I will have you both summoned. I will not listen to him except in your presence ; that, too, is my *sine quâ non.'*

" I bowed profoundly, and the Queen dismissed me with the usual signal. I own, however, that my confidence in the Comte de Saint-Germain was lessened by the coincidence of his coming to Paris with the warning received the day before by Marie-Antoinette. I fancied I saw in it a regular scheme of trickery, and I asked myself if I ought to speak to him about it ; but, considering all, I resolved to be silent, certain that he was prepared beforehand to answer this question.

" M. de Saint-Germain was awaiting me outside. As soon as I perceived him, I stopped my carriage ; he got into it with me, and we returned together to my house. He was present at my dinner, but according to his custom he did not eat ; after this he proposed to go back to Versailles. He would sleep at the inn, he added, and rejoin me the next day. I consented to this, eager as I was to neglect nothing for the success of this business.

**

" We were in my dwelling, then, in quarters which at Versailles were called a suite of apartments, when one of the Queen's pages came to ask me on her Majesty's behalf for the second volume of the book that she had desired me to bring her from Paris. This was the signal agreed upon. I handed the page a volume of some new novel, I know not what, and as soon as he had gone, I followed, accompanied by my lackey.

" We entered through the *cabinets ;* Madame de Misery conducted us into the private room where the Queen was awaiting us. She rose with affable dignity.

" ' Monsieur le Comte,' she said to him, ' Versailles is a place which is familiar to you.'

" ' Madame, for nearly twenty years I was on intimate terms with the late King ; he deigned to listen to me with kindness ; he made use of my poor abilities on several occasions, and I do not think that he regretted having given me his confidence.'

" ' You have wished Madame d'Adhémar to bring you to me ; I have great affection for her and I do not doubt that what you have to tell me deserves listening to.'

" ' The Queen,' answered the Count in a solemn voice, ' will in her wisdom weigh what I am about to confide to her. The Encyclopædist party desire power ; they will only obtain it by the absolute downfall of the clergy, and to ensure this result they will overthrow the monarchy. This party, who seek a chief among the members of the royal family, have turned their eyes on the Duc de Chartres ; this prince will become the tool of men who will sacrifice him when he has ceased to be useful to them ; the crown of France will be offered him, and he will find the scaffold instead of the throne. But before this day of retribution, what cruelties ! what crimes ! Laws will no longer be the protection of the good and the terror of the wicked. It is these last who will seize power with their blood-stained hands ; they will abolish the Catholic religion, the nobility, the magistracy.'

" 'So that nothing but royalty will be left ! ' interrupted the Queen, impatiently.

" 'Not even royalty ! . . . but a greedy republic, whose sceptre will be the axe of the executioner.'

" At these words I could not contain myself, and taking upon me to interrupt the Count in the Queen's presence :

" 'Monsieur ! ' I cried, ' do you think of what you are saying, and before whom you are speaking ? '

" 'In truth,' added Marie-Antoinette, a little agitated, ' these are things that my ears are not accustomed to hear.'

" ' And it is in the gravity of the circumstances that I find this boldness,' coolly replied M. de Saint-Germain. ' I have not come with the intention of paying a homage to the Queen of which she must be weary, but indeed to point out to her the dangers which threaten her crown, if prompt measures are not taken to avert them.'

" ' You are positive, Monsieur,' said Marie-Antoinette, petulantly.

" ' I am deeply grieved to displease your Majesty, but I can only speak the truth.'

" ' Monsieur,' replied the Queen, affecting a playful tone, ' the true, perhaps, may sometimes not be the probable.'

" ' I admit, Madame, that this is a case in point ; but your Majesty will permit me in my turn to remind you that Cassandra foretold the ruin of Troy, and that they refused to believe it. I am Cassandra, France is the kingdom of Priam. Some years yet will pass by in a deceitful calm ; then from all parts of the kingdom will spring up men greedy for vengeance, for power, and for money ; they will overthrow all in their way. The seditious populace and some great members of the State will lend them support ; a spirit of delirium will take possession of the citizens ; civil war will burst out with all its horrors ; it will bring in its train murder, pillage, exile. Then it will be regretted that I was not listened to ; perhaps I shall be asked for again, but the time will be past . . . the storm will have swept all before it.'

"'I confess, Monsieur, that this discourse astonishes me more and more, and did I not know that the late King had an affection for you, and that you had served him faithfully. . . . You wish to speak to the King ? '

"'Yes, Madame.'

"'But without the concurrence of M. de Maurepas ? '

"'He is my enemy ; besides, I rank him among those who will further the ruin of the kingdom, not from malice, but from incapacity.'

"'You are a severe judge of a man who has the approbation of the majority.'

"'He is more than prime minister, Madame, and by right of this he is sure to have flatterers.'

"'If you exclude him from your relations with the King, I fear that you will find it difficult to approach his Majesty, who cannot act without his chief adviser.'

"'I shall be at their Majesties' command as long as they wish to employ me ; but as I am not their subject, all obedience on my part is a gratuitous act.'

"'Monsieur,' said the Queen, who at this period could not treat any matter seriously for long together, ' where were you born ? '

" ' At Jerusalem, Madame.'

" ' And that was . . . when ? '

" ' The Queen will permit me to have a weakness common to many persons. I never like to tell my age ; that brings misfortune.'

" ' As for me, the Royal Almanac does not allow of any illusion about my own. Farewell, Monsieur ; the pleasure of the King shall be communicated to you.'

" This was a dismissal ; we retired, and in returning home with me M. de Saint-Germain said to me :—

" ' I too am about to leave you, Madame, and for a long time, for I do not propose to remain more than four days in France.'

" ' What is it that makes you decide to start so quickly ? '

" ' The Queen will repeat to the King what I have said to her, Louis XVI. will tell it again in his turn to M. de Maurepas, this Minister will draw up a warrant (*lettre de cachet*) against me, and the head of the police will have orders to put it into execution. I know how these things are done, and I have no desire to go to the Bastille.'

" ' What would it matter to you ? You would get out through the key-hole.'

" ' I prefer not to need recourse to a miracle. Farewell, Madame.'

" ' But if the King should summon you ? '

" ' I will return.'

" ' How shall you know it ? '

" ' I have the means of doing so : do not trouble yourself on that point.'

" ' Meanwhile, I shall be compromised ! '

" ' Not so ; farewell.'

" He departed, as soon as he had taken off my livery. I remained greatly troubled. I had told the Queen that in order to be the better able to carry out her wishes, I would not leave the château. . . . Two hours after, Madame de Misery came to seek me on behalf of her Majesty. I augured no good from this eagerness. I found the King with Marie-Antoinette. She appeared to me embarrassed ; Louis XVI., on the contrary, came up to me in a frank way, and took my hand, which he kissed with infinite grace, for he had charming manners when he pleased.

" ' Madame d'Adhémar,' he said to me, ' what have you done with your wizard ? '

" ' The Comte de Saint-Germain, Sire ? He has started for Paris.'

" ' He has seriously alarmed the Queen. Had he previously spoken in the same way to you ? "

" ' Not with so many details.'

" ' I bear no ill-will to you for it, nor does the Queen either, for your intentions are good ; but I blame the stranger for daring to foretell reverses to us which all the four quarters of the globe could not offer in the course of a century. Above all, he is wrong in concealing himself from the Comte de Maurepas, who would know how to lay aside his personal enmities if it were necessary to sacrifice them to the interests of the monarchy. I shall speak to him on the subject, and if he advises me to see Saint-Germain, I shall not refuse to do so. He is credited with intellect and ability ; my grandfather liked his society ; but before granting him a conference, I wished to reassure you as to the possible consequences of the fresh appearance of this mysterious personage. Whatever may happen, you will be held clear.'

" My eyes filled with tears at this striking proof of the kindness of their Majesties, for the Queen spoke to me as affectionately as did the King. I returned calmer, but vexed, nevertheless, at the turn that this affair had taken, and I inwardly congratulated myself that M. de Saint-Germain had foreseen all.

" Two hours later, I was still in my room, absorbed in my own thoughts, when there was a knock at the door of my modest dwelling. I heard an unusual commotion, and almost immediately the two folding doors opened, and Monseigneur le Comte de Maurepas was announced. I rose to receive him with rather more briskness than if it had been the King of France. He came forward with a smiling countenance.

" ' Pardon me, Madame,' he said, ' for the unceremoniousness of my visit ; but I have some enquiries to make of you, and politeness required that I should come to seek you.'

" The courtiers of this period showed an exquisite politeness to women, which was no longer to be found in its purity after the storm which over-turned everything. I replied, as I was bound to do, to M. de Maurepas, and these preliminaries over :—

" ' Well ! ' he resumed, ' our old friend the Comte de Saint-Germain has returned ? . . . He is already at his old tricks, and has recommenced his jugglery.'

" I was about to exclaim ; but stopping me with a gesture of entreaty :—

" ' Believe me,' he added, ' I know the rogue better than you do, Madame. One thing only surprises me ; the years have not spared me, and the Queen declares that the Comte de Saint-Germain presented the appearance of a man of forty. However that may be, we must know whence he has gained this information, so cir-cumstantial, so alarming. . . . He did not give you his address, I will warrant ? '

" ' No, Monsieur le Comte.'

" ' It will be discovered, our police hounds have a keen scent. . . . Further . . . the King thanks you for your zeal. Nothing grievous will befall

Saint-Germain, except the being shut up in the Bastille, where he will be well fed, well warmed, until he condescends to tell us where he has got at so many curious things.'

" At this moment our attention was diverted by the noise made by the opening of the door of my room. . . . It was the Comte de Saint-Germain who entered ! A cry escaped me, while M. de Maurepas hurriedly rose, and I must say that his countenance changed a little. The thaumaturgist, approaching him, said :—

" ' M. le Comte de Maurepas, the King summoned you to give him good advice, and you think only of maintaining your own authority. In opposing yourself to my seeing the Monarch, you are losing the monarchy, for I have but a limited time to give to France and, this time over, I shall not be seen here again until after three consecutive generations have gone down to the grave. I told the Queen all that I was permitted to tell her ; my revelations to the King would have been more complete ; it is unfortunate that you should have intervened between His Majesty and me. I shall have nothing to reproach myself with when horrible anarchy devastates all France. As to these calamities, you will not see them, but to have prepared them will be sufficient memorial of you. . . . Expect no homage from posterity, frivolous and incapable Minister ! You will be ranked among those who cause the ruin of empires.'

" M. de Saint-Germain, having spoken thus without taking breath, turned towards the door again, shut it, and disappeared " [1].

All efforts to find the Count failed !

[1] ADHÉMAR, *op. cit.*, ii., pp. 52–72.

CHAPTER IV

TRAGICAL PROPHECIES

THE most deeply interesting of all the incidents recorded in this diary of Madame d'Adhémar are those which show how M. de St.-Germain strove to warn the Royal Family of the evils which were overshadowing it. He had evidently watched over the unfortunate young Queen from the time of her entry into France. He was the " mysterious adviser " of whom mention is frequently made.

He it was who strove to make the King and Queen understand that M. de Maurepas and their other advisers were wrecking their kingdom. The friend of Royalty, he was yet the one most accused by the Abbé Barruel of leading the Revolution. " Time proves all," and time has allowed the accuser to sink into a well-deserved oblivion, while the accused stands out as true friend and true prophet. Let the voice of the dead woman bear its own witness :—

" The future was darkening ; we were nearing the terrible catastrophe which was about to overwhelm France. The abyss was at our feet ; yet averting our heads, struck with a fatal blindness,

74

we hurried from *fête* to *fête*, from pleasure to pleasure. It was like a kind of frenzy which thrust us gaily on to our destruction. Alas! how can a storm be controlled when one sees it not?

" Meanwhile, from time to time, some troubled or observant minds tried to snatch us from this fatal security. I have already said that the Comte de St.-Germain had tried to unseal the eyes of Their Majesties, by making them perceive the approach of danger; but M. de Maurepas, not wishing the salvation of the country to come from any one but himself, ousted the thaumaturgist, and he re-appeared no more." [1]

The date at which these events were taking place was 1788; the final crash, however, did not culminate until 1793. Madame d'Adhémar is reviewing events and does not in every case put the exact date. The attacks upon the King and Throne were increasing in violence and bitterness year by year, owing to the fatal blindness already alluded to by our writer. The frivolity of the Court increased *pari passu* with the hatred of its enemies. The unfortunate Queen, indeed, did make efforts to understand the condition of affairs, but in vain. Madame d'Adhémar gives some of the details as follows :

" I cannot refrain from copying here, in order

[1] ADHÉMAR, *op. cit.*, iv., 1.

to give an idea of these sad debates [in the National Assembly], a letter written by M. de Sallier, parliamentary adviser to the *Chambres de Requêtes*, and addressed to one of his friends, a member of the parliament at Toulouse. . . . This account was spread abroad and read with avidity; many copies of it were circulated in Paris. Before the original reached Toulouse, it was spoken of in the drawing-room of the Duchesse de Polignac.

" The Queen, turning to me, asked me if I had read it, and requested me to procure it for her. This request caused me real embarrassment ; I wished to obey Her Majesty, and at the same time I feared to displease the ruling Minister ; however my attachment to the Queen prevailed.

" Marie-Antoinette read the article in my presence, and then sighing, ' Ah ! Madame d'Adhémar,' she said, ' how painful all these attacks on the authority of the King are to me ! We are walking on dangerous ground ; I begin to believe that your Comte de St.-Germain was right. We were wrong not to listen to him, but M. de Maurepas imposed a skilful and despotic dictatorship upon us. To what are we coming ? [1]

" . . . The Queen sent for me, and I hastened to her sacred order. She held a letter in her

[1] ADHÉMAR, *op. cit.*, iv., p. 63.

hand. ' Madame d'Adhémar,' she said, ' here is another missive from my unknown. Have you not heard people talking again of the Comte de St.-Germain ? '

" ' No,' I replied ; ' I have not seen him, and nothing has reached me from him.'

" ' This time,' added the Queen, ' the oracle has used the language which becomes him, the epistle is in verse ; it may be bad, but it is not very cheering. You shall read it at your leisure, for I have promised an audience to the Abbé de Ballivières. I wish that my friends could live on good terms ! '

" ' Especially,' I ventured to add, ' as their enemies triumph in their quarrels.'

" ' The unknown says the same as you do ; but who is wrong or right ? '

" ' The Queen may satisfy both parties by means of the first two vacant Bishoprics.'

" ' You are mistaken ; the King will give the episcopal mitre neither to the Abbé d'Erse nor to the Abbé de Ballivières. The protectors of these gentlemen and our Abbé will believe that the ill-will is on my side ; you might, since you are compared to the heroes of Ariosto (the speech of the Baroness de Staël had occurred to the Queen), play the part of peace-maker of the good King Sobrir ; behold the Countess Diana, make her listen to reason.'

" ' I will talk reason to her,' said I, trying to laugh in order to dispel the melancholy of the Queen.

" ' Diana is a spoilt child,' replied Her Majesty, ' however, she loves her friends.'

" ' Yes, Madam, even to showing herself implacable to their enemies !   I will obey the Queen.'

" They came to inform Marie-Antoinette that the Abbé de Ballivières had arrived according to her command.   I passed into the small closet, where having asked Madame Campan for pen, ink, and paper, I copied the following passage, obscure then, but which afterwards became only too clear.

" ' The time is fast approaching when imprudent France,
Surrounded by misfortune she might have spared herself,
Will call to mind such hell as Dante painted.
This day, O Queen ! is near, no more can doubt remain,
A hydra vile and cowardly, with his enormous horns
Will carry off the altar, throne, and Themis ;
In place of common sense, madness incredible
Will reign, and all be lawful to the wicked.
Yea ! Falling shall we see sceptre, censer, scales,
Towers and escutcheons, even the white flag :
Henceforth will all be fraud, murders and violence,
Which we shall find instead of sweet repose.
Great streams of blood are flowing in each town ;
Sobs only do I hear, and exiles see !
On all sides civil discord loudly roars,
And uttering cries on all sides virtue flees,
As from the assembly votes of death arise.
Great God ! who can reply to murderous judges ?
And on what brows august I see the sword descend !

What monsters treated as the peers of heroes !
Oppressors, oppressed, victors, vanquished . . .
The storm reaches you all in turn, in this common wreck,
What crimes, what evils, what appalling guilt,
Menace the subjects, as the potentates !
And more than one usurper triumphs in command,
More than one heart misled is humbled and repents.
At last, closing the abyss and born from a black tomb
There rises a young lily, more happy, and more fair.'

" These prophetic verses, written by a pen we already knew, astonished me. I racked my brains to guess their meaning ; for how could I believe that it was their simplest meaning that I ought to give them ! How imagine, for instance, that it was the King and Queen who would die a violent death, and as the result of iniquitous sentences ? We could not, in 1788, have such clear sight ; it was an impossibility.

" When I returned to the Queen, and no indiscreet person could listen, she said :—

" ' What do you make of these threatening verses ? '

" ' They are dismaying ! But they cannot affect your Majesty. People do say incredible things, follies ; if, however, the prophetic words turn out to be true, they will concern our posterity.'

" ' Pray heaven you speak truly, Madame d'Adhémar,' replied the Queen ; ' however, these are strange experiences. Who is this personage who has taken an interest in me for so many years without making himself known, without seeking any reward, and who yet has always told me the truth ? He now warns me of the overthrow of everything that exists and, if he gives a gleam of hope, it is so distant that I may not reach it.'

" I strove to comfort the Queen ; above all, I told her, she must make her friends live on good terms with each other, and not let their private quarrels be known outside. Marie-Antoinette answered me in these memorable words :—

" ' You fancy that I possess credit or power in our Salon. You are mistaken ; I had the misfortune to believe that a Queen was permitted to have friends. The consequence is that all try to rule me, or to use me for their own personal advantage. I am the centre of a crowd of intrigues, which I have difficulty in avoiding. Everyone complains of my ingratitude. This is not the *rôle* of a Queen of France. There is a very fine verse which I apply to myself, making a change in the reading : " Kings are condemned to magnificence." I should say with more reason : " Kings are condemned to be weary in utter loneliness."

" ' So I should act were I to begin my career again.' " [1]

Madame d'Adhémar does not give any very

---

[1] ADHÉMAR, *op. cit.*, iv., pp. 74–97. The date here mentioned is 1788.

definite dates in her diary, and it is chiefly by the historical episodes, which led up to the final crash, that we are able to mark the passage of time. Passing on from the general events, deeply interesting in themselves, but not bearing on the Comte de St. Germain, we come to the proscription which was passed against the Royalists in 1789, and once more the unfortunate Queen received a warning from her unknown adviser, whose advice alas ! fell on ears too weak to understand. Hearing of the proceedings against the Polignacs, Marie-Antoinette sent to warn the Duchess about her approaching fall. Madame d'Adhémar graphically tells the tale as follows :—

" I arose, and showing the pain that this commission gave me, I went off to Madame de Polignac. I could have wished to find her alone. I met there the Duke, her husband, her sister-in-law, the Count de Vaudreuil and M. l'Abbé de Ballivières. On seeing my solemn look when I entered, my swollen eyes still wet with the tears that had mingled with those of the Queen, they felt that I had come for a sad reason ; the Duchess held out her hand to me.

" ' What have you to tell me ? ' she said ; ' I am prepared for every misfortune.'

" ' Not,' said I, ' for that which is about to burst upon you. Alas ! my sweet friend, bear it with resignation and courage. . . .'

" These words died away on my lips, and the Countess, taking up the words, said :—

" ' You are causing my sister a thousand sufferings by your reticence. Well, Madame, what is the matter ? '

" ' The Queen,' I said, ' in order to avoid the proscription that threatens you—you and yours—wishes you to go for some months to Vienna.'

" ' The Queen drives me away, and you come to tell me ! ' cried the Duchess, rising.

" ' Unjust friend ! ' I answered, ' let me tell you all that remains to be told.'

" Then I went on and repeated word for word what Marie-Antoinette had charged me to tell her.

" There were more cries, more tears, more despairings ; I did not know to whom to listen ; M. de Vaudreuil showed no more firmness than the Polignacs.

" ' Alas ! ' said the Duchess, ' it is my duty to obey, I will certainly depart, since the Queen wills it ; but will she not permit me to repeat verbally my gratitude for her innumerable kindnesses ? '

" ' Never,' said I, ' did she think of your going before she had consoled you ; go then to her chamber, her reception will make amends to you for this apparent disfavour.'

" The Duchess begged me to accompany her,

and I consented. My heart was broken at the sad interview between these friends who loved each other so warmly. It was a flood of complaints, tears, sighs ; they embraced each other so closely that they could not tear themselves apart ; it was truly pitiful to see.

" At this moment a letter was brought to the Queen, curiously sealed ; she glanced at it, shuddered as she looked at me, and said : ' It is from our unknown.'

" ' In truth,' said I, ' it seemed strange to me that he should have remained quiet in such circumstances as these ; besides, he has only anticipated me.'

" Madame de Polignac from her expression appeared eager to know what was so familiar to me.

" A sign that I made let the Queen know this. Her Majesty then proceeded to say :

" ' From the time of my arrival in France, and in every important event in which my interests have been concerned, a mysterious protector has disclosed what I had to fear ; I have told you something of it, and to-day I doubt not that he is advising me what to do.'

" ' Here, Madame d'Adhémar,' she said to me, ' read this letter ; your eyes are less tired than Madame de Polignac's and mine.'

" Alas ! the Queen referred to the tears that

she never ceased to shed. I took the paper and having opened the envelope I read what follows.

" ' Madame—I have been a Cassandra ; my words have fallen on your ears in vain, and you have reached the period of which I informed you. It is no longer a question of tacking but of meeting the storm with thundering energy ; in order to do this and to increase your strength, you must separate yourself from the persons whom you most love so as to remove all pretext from the rebels. Moreover these persons run the risk of their lives ; all the Polignacs and their friends are doomed to death and are pointed out to the assassins who have just murdered the officers of the Bastille and the provost of the merchants. The Comte d'Artois will perish ; they thirst for his blood ; let him take heed to it. I hasten to tell you this, later on I will communicate further with you about it.'

" We were in the stupor which such a menace inevitably causes, when the Comte d'Artois was announced. We all started, and he himself was astounded. He was questioned, and, unable to keep silence, he told us that the Duc de Liancourt had just told him as well as the King, that the men of the Revolution, in order to consolidate it, had made up their minds to take his life (that of the Comte d'Artois), and that of the Duchesse de Polignac, and of the Duc, and also the lives of Messieurs de Vaudreuil, de Vermont, de Guiche, of the Ducs de Broglie, de la Vauguyon, de Castries, the Baron de Breteuil, Messieurs de Villedeuil, d'Amecourt, des Polastrons—in a word a real proscription. . . .[1]

"On returning home, a note was given to me, thus worded :—

"'All is lost, Countess! This sun is the last which will set on the monarchy ; to-morrow it will exist no more, chaos will prevail, anarchy unequalled. You know all I have tried to do to give affairs a different turn ; I have been scorned ; now it is too late.

"'. . . Keep yourself in retirement, I will watch over you ; be prudent, and you will survive the tempest that will have beaten down all. I resist the desire that I have to see you ; what should we say to each other ? You would ask of me the impossible ; I can do nothing for the King, nothing for the Queen, nothing for the Royal Family, nothing even for the Duc d'Orléans, who will be triumphant to-morrow, and who, all in due course, will cross the Capitol to be thrown from the top of the Tarpeian rock. Nevertheless, if you would care very much to meet with an old friend, go to the eight o'clock Mass at the

[1] ADHÉMAR, *op. cit.*, iv., pp. 189–193.

Récollets, and enter the second chapel on the right hand.

      " ' I have the honour to be . . .

          " ' COMTE DE ST.-GERMAIN.'

"At this name, already guessed, a cry of surprise escaped me ; he still living, he who was said to have died in 1784, and whom I had not heard spoken of for long years past—he had suddenly re-appeared, and at what a moment, what an epoch ! Why had he come to France ? Was he then never to have done with life ? For I knew some old people who had seen him bearing the stamp of forty or fifty years of age, and that at the beginning of the eighteenth century !

" It was one o'clock at night when I read his letter ; the hour for the *rendez-vous* was early, so I went to bed ; I slept little, frightful dreams tormented me and, in their hideous grotesqueness, I beheld the future, without however understanding it. As day dawned, I arose worn out. I had ordered my butler to bring me some very strong coffee, and I took two cups of it, which revived me. At half past seven I summoned a sedan chair, and, followed by my confidential old servant, I repaired to the *Récollets*.

" The church was empty ; I posted my Laroche as sentinel and I entered the chapel named ; soon after, and almost before I had collected my thoughts in the presence of God, behold a man approaching. . . . It was himself in person. . . . Yes! with the same countenance as in 1760, while mine was covered with furrows and marks of decrepitude. . . . I stood impressed by it; he smiled at me, came forward, took my hand, kissed it gallantly. I was so troubled that I allowed him to do it in spite of the sanctity of the place.

" ' There you are ! ' I said. ' Where have you come from ? '

" ' I am come from China and Japan. . . .'

" ' Or rather from the other world ! '

" ' Yes, indeed, pretty nearly so ! Ah ! Madame, *down there* (I underline the expression) nothing is so strange as what happens here. How is the monarchy of Louis XIV. disposed of ? You who did not see it cannot make the comparison, but I. . . .'

" ' I have caught you, man of yesterday ! '

" ' Who does not know the history of this great reign ? And Cardinal Richelieu, if he were reborn, it would send him mad. What ! not rule ! What did I tell you, and the Queen too ? that M. de Maurepas would let everything be lost, because he compromised everything. I was Cassandra, or a prophet of evil, and now how do you stand ? '

" ' Ah ! Comte, your wisdom will be useless.'

" ' Madame, he who sows the wind reaps the whirlwind. Jesus said so in the Gospel, perhaps not before me, but at any rate His words remain written, and people could only have profited by mine.'

" ' Again ! ' I said, trying to smile, but he without replying to my exclamation said :—

" ' I have written it to you, *I can do nothing, my hands are tied by a stronger than myself.* There are periods of time when to retreat is impossible, others when *He* has pronounced and the decree will be executed. *Into this we are entering.*'[1]

" ' Will you see the Queen ? '

" ' No, she is doomed.'

" ' Doomed ! To what ? '

" ' To death ! '

" Oh, this time I could not keep back a cry, I rose on my seat, my hands repulsed the Comte, and in a trembling voice I said :

" ' And you too ! you ! what, you too ! '

" ' Yes, I——I, like Cazotte.'

" ' You know. . . .'

" ' What you do not even suspect. Return to the Palace, go and tell the Queen to take heed to herself, that this day will be fatal to her ; there is a plot, murder is premeditated.'

" ' You fill me with horror, but the Comte d'Estaing has promised.'

---

[1] The italics are in the original.

" ' He will take fright, and will hide himself.'

" ' But M. de Lafayette. . . .'

" ' A balloon puffed out with wind ! Even now they are settling what to do with him, whether he shall be instrument or victim ; by noon all will be decided.'

" ' Monsieur,' I said, ' you could render great services to our Sovereigns if you would.'

" ' And if I cannot ? '

" ' How ? '

" ' Yes ; if I cannot ? I thought I should not be listened to. The hour of repose is past, and the decrees of Providence must be fulfilled.'

" ' In plain words, what do they want ? '

" ' The complete ruin of the Bourbons ; they will expel them from all the thrones they occupy, and in less than a century they will return to the rank of simple private individuals in their different branches.'

" ' And France ? '

" ' Kingdom, Republic, Empire, mixed Governments, tormented, agitated, torn ; from clever tyrants she will pass to others who are ambitious without merit. She will be divided, parcelled out, cut up ; and these are no pleonasms that I use, the coming times will bring about the overthrow of the Empire ; pride will sway or abolish distinctions, not from virtue but from vanity, and it is through vanity that they will come back to them. The French, like children playing with handcuffs and slings, will play with titles, honours, ribbons ; everything will be a toy to them, even to the shoulder-belt of the National Guard ; the greedy will devour the finances. Some fifty millions now form a deficit, in the name of which the Revolution is made. Well ! under the dictatorship of the philanthropists, the rhetoricians, the fine talkers, the State debt will exceed several thousand millions ! '

" ' You are a terrible prophet ! When shall I see you again ? '

" ' Five times more ; do not wish for the sixth.'

" I confess that a conversation so solemn, so gloomy, so terrifying, inspired me with little wish to continue it. M. de St.-Germain oppressed my heart like a night-mare, it is strange how much we change with age, how we look with indifference, even disgust, on those whose presence formerly charmed us. I found myself in this condition under present circumstances ; besides, the immediate danger of the Queen pre-occupied me. I did not sufficiently urge the Count, perhaps if I had entreated him he would have come to her ; there was a pause, and then, resuming the conversation :—

" ' Do not let me detain you longer,' he said ; ' there is already disturbance in the city. I am like Athalie, *I wished to see and I have seen.* Now

I will take up my part again and leave you   I
have a journey to take to Sweden ; a great crime
is brewing there, I am going to try to prevent it.
His Majesty Gustavus III. interests me, he is
worth more than his renown.'

" ' And he is menaced ? '

" ' Yes ; no longer will " happy as a king " be
said, and still less as a queen.'

" ' Farewell, then, Monsieur ; in truth I wish I
had not listened to you.'

" ' Thus it is ever with us truthful people ;
deceivers are welcomed, but fie upon whoever
says that which will come to pass ! Farewell,
Madame ; *au revoir !* '

" He departed ; I remained absorbed in deep
meditation, not knowing whether I ought to
inform the Queen of this visit or not ; I decided
to wait till the end of the week, and to keep
silence if it teemed with misfortunes. I arose at
last and when I had found Laroche again I asked
him if he had seen the Comte de St.-Germain as
he went out.'

" ' The Minister, Madame ? '

" ' No, he has long been dead ; the other.'

" ' Ah ! the clever conjuror ? '

" ' No, Madame ; did Madame la Comtesse meet
him ? '

" ' He went out just now, he passed close to
you.'

" ' I must have been distracted, for I did not notice him.'

" ' It is impossible, Laroche, you are joking.'

" ' The worse the times are the more respectful I am to Madame.'

" ' What ! by this door—close to you—he has passed ? '

" ' I do not mean to deny it, but he did not strike my eye.'

" ' Then he had made himself invisible ! I am lost in astonishment '."[1]

These are the last words that the Countess d'Adhémar writes in connection with the Comte de St. Germain or that friend who had tried so vainly to save them from the storm which was then raging on all sides. One important note which has been already noticed may, however, here again be fitly quoted. It is evidently from the pen of the biographer that we get this important little memo, which is as follows :

" Note written by the hand of the Countess, fastened with a pin to the original MS. and dated the 12th May, 1821. She died in 1822. " I saw M. de St. Germain again, and always to my unspeakable surprise : at the assassination of the Queen ; at the coming of the 18th Brumaire ; the day following the death of the Duc d'Enghien ; in the month of January, 1813 ; and on the eve of

[1] ADHÉMAR, *op. cit.*, iv., pp. 254–261.

the murder of the Duc de Berri. I await the sixth visit when God wills.' "

Thus does a voice from the dead contradict the malicious diatribes made against this teacher, and also refute the unfounded assertions about his death in 1784, made by Dr. Biester of Berlin, which have been already fully noted. Perhaps the most interesting passages are those which give the utterances of the Comte de St. Germain with regard to the future of France. It is now a hundred and thirty years since those words were uttered, and we can see that they have been accurately correct in every detail. The Bourbons are now but a private family. The honour of France has been wrecked by those who had arrogated to themselves positions of honour and trust, in which their moral characters were not able to stand the strain ; cases may be cited as instances illustrating, but too clearly, the truth of the sorrowful forecast made by the Mystic Messenger of the last century. He might have fitly quoted the words of the Prophet forerunner, " I am the voice of one crying in the wilderness." [1] But, alas for France, neither prophecies nor warnings availed her ; slowly and sadly has the wheel of her life turned round, proving the veracity and accuracy of that prophet who was sent to warn her of the doom to come.

[1] *Isaiah*, xl. 3.

CHAPTER V

POLITICAL WORK

THE earliest definite hint of any political work on the part of the Comte de St. Germain is from the pen of Madame d'Adhémar.[1]

When sketching the portraits of those who were received into intimacy by Louis XV. at Versailles, she says : " The King was also much attached to the Duchesse de Choiseul, *née* Crozat ; her simplicity, her frankness, more virtues than were necessary to make a success at Versailles, had triumphed over the drawback of her birth, and she was frequently present at the suppers in the smaller apartments. One man also had long enjoyed this favour, the celebrated and mysterious Comte de St. Germain, my friend who has not been rightly known, and to whom I shall devote some pages when I have to speak of Cagliostro. From 1749, the King employed him on diplomatic missions and he acquitted himself honourably in them."

This passage would remain incomprehensible, unless we glance briefly at the history of the

[1] *Souvenirs sur Marie-Antoinette*, i., p. 8

period. Dark and stormy is the scene on which we enter ; difficult indeed is it to disentangle the knotted web of European politics which enmeshed the various nations. Austria and France had signed in 1756 an offensive and defensive alliance, especially directed against England and Prussia ; Russia was with them ; during the Seven Years' War the throne of Prussia tottered more than once, until the Austrians were defeated at Torgau in 1760. Poland, that " Niobe of Nations," was watching the clouds gather slowly on her horizon ; racked within by strife stirred up by Russia, she struggled vainly against the stronger Powers ; her day was slowly ending. England, at war in America and with France, striving also to conquer India, was also a centre of discord. All Europe was in dissension.

Into this arena of combat the Comte de St. Germain was asked to step by the King of France, in order to make that peace which his Ministers—involved in their own plans—could not, or would not, make.

Louis XV. was practically the originator of the whole system of secret diplomacy, which in the eighteenth century seems to stand out as a new departure in the diplomatic political world. The Gordian knot which could not be disentangled, Louis XV. tried to cut ; hence we find the King of France employing secret agents, men who could be trusted with delicate missions, men foredoomed to bear the blame of failure, fated never to be crowned with the palm of success.

Outside the various Foreign Offices, or beyond the pale of their secret archives, it is very little known that the Comte de St. Germain had any diplomatic mission whatsoever. In many histories and memoirs there is no mention of this phase of his life; therefore it is necessary to cite such writers as are available to bear their testimony on this point.

Not least amongst these stands Voltaire, the sceptic, who in his voluminous correspondence with Frederick of Prussia says, April 15th, 1758 : " Your ministers are doubtless likely to have a better outlook at Breda than I ; M. le Duc de Choiseul, M. de Kaunitz, and M. Pitt do not tell me their secret. It is said to be only known by a M. de St. Germain, who supped formerly at Trent with the Council Fathers, and who will probably have the honour of seeing your Majesty in the course of fifty years. He is a man who never dies, and who knows everything."[1]

The allusion " supped at Trent " is a reference to the gossip which originated from Lord Gower's impersonation and misrepresentation of M. de St. Germain, of which mention has already been

[1] VOLTAIRE, Œuvres. Lettre cxviii., ed. Beuchot, lviii., p. 360.

made. The important point in this letter is that Voltaire refers to a political connection of M. de St. Germain with the Prime Ministers of England, France and Austria, as if he were in the intimate council of these leaders. The Baron de Gleichen gives some details in his memoirs, and as he became later deeply interested in the mystical work of the Comte de St. Germain, his version is of much value, giving as it does an insight into some of the complications in France. He writes : " The Marshal [de Belle-Isle] was incessantly intriguing to get a special treaty of peace made with Prussia, and to break up the alliance between France and Austria, on which rested the credit of the Duc de Choiseul. Louis XV. and Madame de Pompadour wished for this special treaty of peace. . . . The Marshal drew up the instructions ; the King delivered them himself with a cipher to M. de St. Germain." [1]

Thus, then, is the mission duly signed and sealed by the King himself, but, as we shall see, even the royal protection could not avert the suspicion and distrust which so unpleasant a position naturally incurred, and when M. de St. Germain arrived at the Hague he came into collision with M. d'Affry, [2] the accredited Ambassador from France.

[1] GLEICHEN (C. H. Baron de) *Mémoires*. Paris, 1868, xi., p. 130.

[2] Ludwig Augustin d'Affry, a Swiss, born 1715 at Ver-

S.G. H

Before entering on the ambassadorial despatches there are a few words from Herr Barthold to be noticed, giving an interesting account of this diplomatic mission ; he—after criticising somewhat severely, and with good reason, the unreliable statements about our philosopher made by the Marquise de Créqui and the Markgräfin von Anspach—goes on : " But of this mysterious mission of the Adept, as financier to the crown and diplomatic Agent, to which he was initiated, not at the ministerial desk, but in the laboratory of Chambord, she makes no mention. Nor has this point—so essential to the understanding of the way business was conducted in France, both in Cabinet and State, at this period—ever been much commented on. About this time we find St. Germain at the Hague, evidently on a private mission, where the Comte d'Affry was French Ambassador, but the two had no relations with each other. Voltaire, who is generally a good reporter, ascribes the Comte's appearance to the Secret Treaty of Peace."[1] The date mentioned by this author is not quite accurate, as we shall see.

That the Duc de Choiseul was profoundly

sailles, Ambassador at the Hague in 1755, became in 1780 Colonel of the Swiss Guard, died in 1793 at his castle Barthelemy in Waadt.

[1] BARTHOLD, *Die Geschichtlichen Persönlichkeiten*. Berlin, 1846, ii., p. 81.

annoyed when this information reached him, is to be understood ; his pet schemes were in jeopardy, his intrigues against England were on the eve of failure ; it appears that M. d'Affry "bitterly reproached M. de Choiseul for having sacrificed an old friend of his father, and the dignity of an Ambassador, to the ambition of making a Treaty of Peace under his very eyes without informing him of it, through an obscure foreigner. M. de Choiseul immediately sent back the courier, ordering M. d'Affry to make a peremptory demand to the States-General to deliver up M. de St. Germain and, that being done, to send him bound hand and foot to the Bastille. The next day M. de Choiseul produced in Council the despatch of M. d'Affry ; he then read his own reply ; then, casting his eyes haughtily on his colleagues, and fixing them alternatively round on King and on M. de Belle-Isle, he added : ' If I did not give myself time to take the orders of the King, it is because I am convinced that no one here would be bold enough to desire to negotiate a Treaty of Peace without the know-ledge of Your Majesty's Minister for Foreign Affairs ! ' He knew that this Prince had estab-lished, and always maintained, the principle, that the Minister of one department should not meddle with the affairs of another. It turned out as he had foreseen. The King cast down his eyes like a guilty person, the Marshal dared not say a word, and M. de Choiseul's action was approved ; but M. de St. Germain escaped him. Their Highnesses, having made good their assent, despatched a large body of guards to arrest M. de St. Germain, who, having been privately warned, fled to England. I have some grounds for believing that he soon left it again to go to St. Petersburg."[1]

No better account could be given than this, by one present at the French Cabinet Council, of the way in which Louis XV., weak and irresolute, allowed his arrangements to be cancelled without a word. Passing, however, rapidly on to follow the events at the Hague, we next have some interesting despatches from M. de Kauderbach, Minister from the Saxon Court at the Hague, wherein he recounts much that has already been given in these pages in praise of the Comte de St. Germain, of his powers and knowledge and then goes on to say : " I had a long conversation with him on the causes of the troubles of France, and on the changes in the choice of Minister in this kingdom. This, Monseigneur, is what he said to me on the subject : ' The radical evil is the monarch's want of firmness. Those who surround him, knowing his extreme good nature, abuse it, and he is surrounded only by

[1] GLEICHEN (C. H. Baron de) *Mémoires*, xi., pp. 131, 132.

creatures placed by the Brothers Pâris,[1] who alone cause all the trouble of France. It is they who corrupt everything, and thwarted the plans of the best citizen in France, the Marshal de Belle-Isle. Hence the disunion and jealousy amongst the Ministers, who seem all to serve a different monarch. All is corrupted by the Brothers Pâris ; perish France, provided they may attain their object of gaining eight hundred millions ! Unhappily the King has not so much sagacity as good nature ; he is not, therefore, aware of the malice of the people around him who, knowing his lack of firmness, are solely occupied in flattering his foible, and through it are ever preferably listened to. The same defect as to firmness is found in the mistress. She knows the evil and has not courage to remedy it.' It is he then, M. de St. Germain, who will undertake to cure it radically ; he takes upon himself to put down by his influence and operations in Holland the two names so prejudicial to the State, which have hitherto been regarded as indispensably necessary. Hearing him speak with so much freedom, one must look upon him either as a man sure of his ground, or else as the greatest fool in the world. I could entertain your Excellency much longer with this singular man and with his knowledge of physics,

[1] The Brothers Pâris-Duverney were the great financiers, the bank monarchs, in the time of Louis XV.

did I not fear to weary you with tales which must seem rather romantic than real."[1]

The Saxon diplomatist, from whose despatches these extracts are gathered, very shortly changed his friendly tone, on finding that the Duc de Choiseul did not favour the plans of Louis XV. ; the self-respecting diplomat then began to disparage the man whom so lately he had lauded as a prodigy, hence the next despatch is amusingly different in tone, and runs as follows :

" April 24th, 1760. I have this moment heard that the courier whom the Comte d'Affry received last Monday brought him an order to demand from the State the arrest and extradition of the famous St. Germain as a dangerous character, and one with whom his most Christian Majesty has reason to be dissatisfied. M. d'Affry, having communicated this order to the *Pensionnaire*, this Minister of State reported it to the Council of Deputy Commissioners for the province of Holland, an assembly of which the Comte de Bentinck is President. The latter gave the man warning, and made him start for England. The day before his departure, St. Germain was four hours with the English Minister. He boasted of being authorised to make peace."

Later on, in another despatch, this wary dip-

[1] TAILLANDIER, SAINT-RENÉ, *Un Prince Allemand du XVIII. Siècle. Revue des deux Mondes*, lxi., pp. 896, 897.

lomatist returns once more to the attack. " The adventurer gave himself here the airs of a secret negotiator, selected by the Marshal de Belle-Isle, from whom he showed letters in which there were in fact some traces of confidence. He wished it to be understood that the principles of the Marshal, differing from those of M. de Choiseul, and more in accordance with the inclination of Mme. de Pompadour, were warmly in favour of peace ; he darkened the picture, painting in the strongest colours the cabals, the difficulties and the dissension that he declared reigned in France, and by these flatteries he thought to gain the confidence of the English party. On the other hand he had written to the Marshal de Belle-Isle, that M. d'Affry knew not how to appreciate or carry out the plans of the Comte de Bentinck-Rhoon, who was a man of the best intentions in the world, and desired only to make himself useful to France in order to promote the success of her negotiations with England. These letters were sent back to M. d'Affry, with a command to forbid St. Germain to meddle with any transactions, on pain of expiating his rashness for the rest of his days in a dungeon on his return to France."[1]

Truly ludicrous is the difference in the tone of these documents ; M. de St. Germain was endea-

[1] TAILLANDIER, *op. cit.*, p. 897.

vouring to carry out the wishes of the King, and trying to help an exhausted country ; these efforts for peace were frustrated by de Choiseul, who had his own schemes to forward with Austria. Nothing more natural could have occurred than that the new helper should be attacked by the opposite party.

It is evident, from the paper cited, that M. de St. Germain was in the confidence of the Marshal de Belle-Isle—who also wanted peace— for the Saxon Ambassador uses the phrase " some traces of confidence," when speaking of the correspondence he had seen and the evidence of confidence he was forced to admit. From this distance of time we can see that the picture of France sketched by M. de St. Germain was by no means too dark : France impoverished, rushing wildly on to greater ruin, the end of which was to be a scene of blood and butchery. He who had the power of seeing the evil days that were drawing so steadily nigh, could he paint that picture too darkly, when endeavouring to stay the ruin of fair France ?

But we must take up some other threads of this tangled skein. The King of Prussia was, at this period, in Freyberg, and his own agent, M. d'Edelsheim, had just arrived in London to confer with the English Ministers ; the following account is given later by Frederick II. of the condition of affairs : " On his arrival in that city [London], another political phenomenon appeared there, a man whom no one has been able to understand. He was known under the name of the Comte de St. Germain. He had been employed by France, and was even so high in favour with Louis XV., that this Prince had thought of giving him the Palace of Chambord " (De l'hiver de 1759 à 1760).[1]

The mission of M. d'Edelsheim is not clearly stated, but we find that not only did M. de St. Germain have to leave London, failing to bring about the peace so sorely desired, but that the Prussian agent fared even worse ; the details are given by Herr Barthold [2] : " The Prussian negotiator . . . returning from London *viâ* Holland to fetch his luggage from Paris, was induced to remain a few days with the Bailly de Froulay, and then, receiving a *Lettre de Cachet*, he was put into the Bastille. Choiseul assured the prisoner that it was only by these means that he could silence the suspicions of the Imperial Minister, Stahremberg, but this ' *scène indécente* ' was simply a trap to get hold of the Baron's papers. Choiseul, however, found nothing and told him to decamp, advising him on his leaving Turin

---

[1] FREDERIC II., Roi de Prusse, *Œuvres Posthumes*. Berlin, 1788, iii., p. 73.

[2] BARTHOLD, *op. cit.*, pp. 93, 94.

not to re-enter the kingdom. Frederick takes care not to find fault with his agent, who through over-zeal had drawn discredit on himself in Paris ; on the other hand, one may conclude that it was he who, through an article in the London *Chronicle*, succeeded in frustrating St. Germain's project."

In this extraordinary maze of secret negotiations it is difficult to find the truth, for in the work just cited we hear that St. Germain was seen in the Bois de Boulogne in May, 1761. When the Marquise d'Urfé informed the Duc de Choiseul of his presence in Paris that Prime Minister replied : " Je n'en suis pas surpris, puisqu'il a passé la nuit dans mon cabinet." [1] This informant proceeds : " Casanova is therefore satisfied that de Choiseul had only pretended to be annoyed with M. de St. Germain, so as to make it easier for him to be sent to London as agent ; Lord Halifax however saw through the plan."

This would indeed be one method of cutting the political entanglement of France !—an intrigue of a pronounced sort arranged by the King, apparently without the knowledge of his chief Minister, in order to arrive at a peace for which the whole country pined. In this difficult situation the Marshal de Belle-Isle selected the Comte de

[1] BARTHOLD, *op. cit.*, p. 94.

The Southern side of the Royal Castle of Chambord, where the Comte de St. Germain lived in 1758 by permission of Louis XV.

St. Germain as the messenger of peace. Alas! missions of peace rarely result in anything but discomfort and slander for the bearer of the message, and the history of the world recorded one more failure, a failure caused by the ambitions of the political leaders.

Leaving now the condition of affairs in France and passing on to England, we find some very interesting correspondence between General Yorke, the English representative at the Hague, and Lord Holdernesse in London. By especial permission from the Foreign Office we have been kindly permitted to make use of these extracts. The full correspondence is too lengthy to print in the limited space permissible in these pages. The first despatch is from General Yorke to the Earl of Holdernesse; it is dated March 14th, 1760, and gives the full account of a long interview between the Comte de St. Germain and himself. The former claims, he says, to have been sent by France to negotiate concerning the Peace, but says that Mons. d'Affry is not in the secret. The answer to this document comes from "Whitehall, March 21st, 1760," and is from Lord Holdernesse to General Yorke; in this he directs the latter "to tell M. de St. Germain that by the King's orders he cannot discuss the subject with him unless he produces some authentic proof of his being employed with the consent and knowledge of the French King." In the next despatch, dated Whitehall, March 28th, 1760, " the King directs that the same answer should be returned to Mons. d'Affry as has already been given to M. de St. Germain. The King thinks it probable that M. de St. Germain was authorised to talk to General Yorke in the manner he did, and that his commission is unknown to the Duc de Choiseul."

The insight of George III. in this case is remarkable, unless in his private correspondence with Louis XV. some hint as to the real condition of things may have been given by one king to the other. In any case the fact remains that owing to M. de Choiseul the Treaty of Peace was not arranged ; and, as we have seen, M. de St. Germain passed on from England to Russia. Turning now to some other witnesses, we find M. Thiébault in his memoirs saying : " While this singular man was at Berlin, I ventured one day to speak of him to the French envoy, the Marquis de Pons Saint-Maurice ; I privately expressed to him my great surprise that this man should have held private and intimate relations with persons of high rank, such as the Cardinal de Bernis, from whom he had, it was said, confidential letters, written at the time when the Cardinal held the portfolio for Foreign Affairs, etc. ; on this last point the envoy made me no reply." [1] This passage implies other diplomatic missions, of which no details are to be found.

Another writer, who has also been quoted, makes an important statement to the effect that when M. de St. Germain was in Leipzig the Graf Marcolini offered him a high public position at Dresden. Our philosopher was at Leipzig in 1776, under the name of Chevalier Weldon, and did not at all conceal the fact that he was a Prince Ragotzy. This informant says : " The Lord High Chamberlain, Graf Marcolini, came from Dresden to Leipzig and made to the Comte—in the name of the Court—certain promises ; M. de St. Germain refused them, but he came in 1777 to Dresden, where he had much intercourse with the Prussian Ambassador, von Alvensleben." [2] This statement can be corroborated by the writer of the life of Graf Marcolini, which has been carefully compiled from the secret archives of the Saxon Court (with especial permission) by the Freiherr O'Byrn.

The Graf Marcolini was a man renowned for his integrity and upright character ; his biographer says : " Considering the strong opposition shown by the Graf Marcolini to the swindling in the Schröpfer affair, the sympathy he extended

[1] THIÉBAULT, D., op. cit., iv., p. 84 ; 3rd ed.
[2] HEZEKIEL, G., Abenteuerliche Gesellen, i., p. 46. Berlin, 1862.

to the Comte de St. Germain on his arrival in Saxony is all the more wonderful. . . . Graf Marcolini repaired to Leipzig with the intention of interviewing St. Germain on hearing of his arrival under the name of Welldoun, October 1776 . . . the meeting resulted in the Graf offering St. Germain an important post in Dresden if he would render a great service to the State ; the ' Wonder Man ' however refused these offers." [1]

Nowhere are to be found the details of any of these diplomatic missions ; we can only gather the fragments and, piecing them together, the fact stands clearly proved, that from Court to Court, among kings, princes, and ambassadors, the Comte de St. Germain was received and known, was trusted as friend, and by none feared as enemy.

[1] O'BYRN, F. A., *Camillo, Graf Marcolini : Eine Biographische Skizze.* Dresden, 1877.

CHAPTER VI

IN THE "MITCHELL PAPERS"

THE diplomatic correspondence which forms almost the whole of this paper is practically an appendix to the last chapter. The details given are interesting and important links in that chain of events which brought M. de St. Germain to England. Chance, good-fortune, or some beneficent power gave the clue to these hidden records.

The "Mitchell Papers," in which these interesting letters have been so long concealed, have never yet been entirely published. It appears that George III. requested that these documents should not be made public during his life, and they were accordingly consigned to the personal care of Mr. Planta, Keeper of the British Museum.

This correspondence was bought by the Trustees of the Museum from Sir William Forbes, the heir of Sir Andrew Mitchell, who had been Envoy at Berlin during the time that all these events took place. A certain portion of the record of his diplomatic career was published by Mr. Bisset in 1850 ; no mention, however, was made of M. de

St. Germain, and the letters which treated of him were unnoticed.

There appears, curiously enough, to have been a " conspiracy of silence " amongst the diplomatists and writers of this period and later, for it is a constantly recurring experience to find all reference to our philosopher carefully excluded, even in cases where the original sources contain much information about him.

A striking instance of such omission is found by searching the different editions of works in which M. de St. Germain is mentioned ; the later editions usually exclude the information given in the earlier ones. Notably may this be seen in a work [1] already referred to, by Dr. Carl von Weber, Keeper of the Saxon Archives in Dresden. In the first edition of this work there is a long article on M. de St. Germain, which is not to be found in the later editions of these volumes. Instances might be easily multiplied of this steady omission wherever possible.

Now the Foreign Office records contain a voluminous correspondence, which is by permission at length being gathered together ; this includes the letters of Prince Galitzin, who was at the period Russian Minister in England. All the

---

[1] WEBER (Dr. Carl von), *Aus vier Jahrhunderten. Mittheilungen aus dem Haupt-Staats-Archive zu Dresden*, Leipzig, 1857.

correspondence is marked " secret," and can only be seen when sanctioned.

The British Museum records have no such restrictions, hence the documents which make up this paper have been copied without delay. The first letter appears to show that Lord Holdernesse already knew of M. de St. Germain, but no facts have so far been found on this point. The language is quaint, and the style somewhat heavy, but the contents present a page of history well worth our study.

It must be remembered that the mission undertaken by the Comte de St. Germain was a secret one, and that he had to disguise how far he was in the confidence of Louis XV. ; with this point in mind it will be easier to understand the difficulties in which he was involved. Turning now to the documents, we find that the first letter is from General Yorke.

MITCHELL PAPERS, VOL. XV.

LD. HOLDERNESSE'S DESPATCHES, etc. 1760 ; 6818, PLUT. P. L., CLXVIII. I. (12).

Copy of General Yorke's letter to the Earl of Holdernesse ; Hague, March 14th, 1760. In Lord Holdernesse's of the 21st, 1760. Secret.
" Hague, March 14th, 1760.

" MY LORD,

" My present situation is so very delicate,

that I am sensible I stand in need of the utmost indulgence, which I hope I shall continue to find from His Majesty's unbounded goodness, and that your Lordship is convinced that whatever I say, or do, has no other motive but the advantage of the King's service. As it has pleased His Majesty to convey to France His sentiments in general upon the situation of affairs in Europe, and to express by me His wishes for restoring the public tranquillity, I suppose the Court of Versailles imagines the same channel may be the proper one for addressing itself to that of England. This is, at least, the most natural way of accounting for the pains taken by France to employ anybody to talk to me.

" Your Lordship knows the history of that extraordinary man, known by the name of Count St. Germain, who resided some time in England where he did nothing ; and has within these two or three years resided in France where he has been upon the most familiar footing with the French King, Madame Pompadour, M. de Belle-isle, etc. ; which has procured him a grant of the Royal Castle of Chambord,[1] and has enabled him to make a certain figure in that country.

" He appeared, for some days, at Amsterdam where he was much caressed and talked of, and upon the marriage of Princess Caroline alighted

[1] An Apartment in the Castle : v. Appendix I.

at the Hague. The same curiosity created the same attention to him here. His volubility of tongue furnished him with hearers ; his freedom upon all subjects, all kinds of suppositions— among which his being sent about Peace not the least.

" M. d'Affry treats him with respect and attention but is very jealous of him and did not so much as renew my acquaintance with him. He called, however, at my door. I returned his visit ; and yesterday he desired to speak with me in the afternoon, but did not come as he appointed, and therefore he renewed his application this morning and was admitted. He began immediately to run on about the bad state of France— their want of Peace—their desire to make it, and his own particular ambition to contribute to an event so desirable for humanity in general ; he ran on about his predilection for England and Prussia which he pretended at present made him a good friend to France.

" As I knew so much of this man, and did not choose to enter into conversation without being better informed, I affected at first to be very grave and dry—told him that those affairs were too delicate to be treated between persons who had no vocation and therefore desired to know what he meant. I suppose this style was irksome to him, for immediately afterwards he produced to me, by way of credentials, two letters from Marshal Belleisle, one dated the 4th, the other the 26th of February. In the first he sends him the French King's passport *en blanc* for him to fill up ; in the second he expresses great impatience to hear from him, and in both runs out in praises of his zeal, his ability, and the hopes that are founded upon what he is gone about. I have no doubt of the authenticity of those letters.

" After perusing them, and some commonplace compliments, I asked him to explain himself, which he did as follows :—the King, the Dauphin, Madame Pompadour, and all the Court and Nation, except the Duke Choiseul and Mr. Berrier, desire peace with England. They can't do otherwise, for their interior requires it. They want to know the real sentiments of England, they wish to make up matters with some honour. M. d'Affry is not in the secret, and the Duke Choiseul is so Austrian that he does not tell all he receives ; but that signifies nothing, for he will be turned out. Madame Pompadour is not Austrian, but is not firm, because she does not know what to trust to ; if she is sure of Peace, she will become so. It is she, and the Marshal Belleisle, with the French King's knowledge, who send St. Germain as the forlorn hope. Spain is not relied upon ; that is a turn given by the Duke Choiseul, and they don't pretend to expect much good from that quarter. This, and much more, was advanced by this political Adventurer. I felt myself in a great doubt whether I should enter into conversation ; but as I am convinced he is really sent, as he says, I thought I should not be disapproved if I talked in general terms. I therefore told him that the King's desire for Peace was sincere, and there could be no doubt of it, since we had made the proposal in the middle of our success which had much increased since ; that with our Allies, the affair was easy, without them impossible ; and that France knew our situation too well, to want such information from me ; that as to particulars, we must be convinced of their desire, before they could be touched upon, and that, besides, I was not informed ; I talked of the dependence of France upon the two Empresses, and the disagreeable prospect before them even if the King of Prussia was unfortunate, but declined going any farther than the most general, though the most positive, assurance of a desire for Peace on His Majesty's part.

" As the conversation grew more animated I asked him what France had felt the most for in her losses, whether it was Canada ? No, he said, for they felt it had cost them thirty-six millions, and brought them no return. Guadaloupe ? They would never stop the Peace for that, as they would have sugar enough without it. The East Indies ? That he said was the same place, as it was connected with all their money affairs. I asked him what they said of Dunkirk ? He made no difficulty to demolish it, and that I might depend upon it. He then asked me what we thought about Minorca ? I answered, that we had forgot it, at least, nobody ever mentioned it ; that, says he, I have told them over and over again, and they are embarrassed with the expense.

" This is the material part of what passed in the course of three hours' conversation which I promised to relate ; he begged the secret might be kept, and he should go to Amsterdam, and to Rotterdam, till he knew whether I had any answer ; which I neither encouraged, nor discouraged him from expecting.

" I humbly hope His Majesty will not disapprove what I have done ; it is not easy to conduct oneself under such circumstances, though I can as easily break off all intercourse as I have taken it up.

" The King seemed desirous to open the door for Peace, and France seems in great want of it ; the opportunity looks favourable, and I shall wait for orders before I stir a step farther. A General Congress seems not to their taste, and they seem willing to go farther than they care to say, but they would be glad of some offer; and H. M. C. M., and the Lady, are a little indolent in taking a resolution.

"I have, etc.

"J. YORKE."

It is clear that the English Envoy found himself in a difficult position; the credentials of the Comte de St. Germain were sufficiently good to ensure a hearing, but he was not an accredited Minister. George II. seems to have understood the complication to some extent, as it would appear from the answer sent at his command, by Lord Holdernesse, which runs as follows:

Copy of letter from the Earl of Holdernesse to Major-General Yorke. Secret.

"*Whitehall, March 21st,* 1760.

"SIR,

"I have the pleasure to acquaint you that His Majesty entirely approves your conduct in the conversation you had with Count St. Germain, of which you give an account in your secret letter of the 14th.

"The King particularly applauds your caution of not entering into conversation with him, till he produced two letters from Marshal Belleisle, which you rightly observe were a sort of credential; as you talked to him only in general terms, and in a way conformable to your former instructions, no detriment could arise to His Majesty's service were everything you said publicly known.

" His Majesty does not think it unlikely that Count St. Germain may really have been authorised (perhaps even with the knowledge of His Most Christian Majesty) by some Persons of weight in the Councils of France to talk as he has done, and no matter what the channel is if a desirable end can be obtained by it. But there is no venturing farther conversations between one of the King's accredited Ministers and such a person as this St. Germain is, according to his present appearance. What you say will be authentic ; whereas, St. Germain will be disavowed with very little ceremony whenever the Court of France finds it convenient. And by his own account his commission is not only unknown to the French Ambassador at the Hague, but even to the Minister for Foreign Affairs at Versailles, who, though threatened with the same fate that befel the Cardinal Bernis, is still the apparent Minister.

" It is therefore His Majesty's pleasure that you should acquaint Count St. Germain that in answer to the letters you wrote me in consequence of your conversation with him, you are directed to say, that you cannot talk with him upon such interesting subjects unless he produces some authentic proof of his being really employed with the knowledge and consent of His Most Christian Majesty. But at the same time you may add, that the King, ever ready to prove the sincerity and purity of his intentions to prevent the farther effusion of Christian blood, will be ready to open Himself on the conditions of a Peace, if the Court of France will employ a person duly authorised to negotiate on that subject ; provided always, that it be previously explained and understood, that in case the two Crowns shall come to agree on the terms of their Peace, that the Court of France shall expressly and confidentially agree that His Majesty's Allies, and *nommément* the King of Prussia, are to be comprehended in the *accomodement à faire.*

" It is unnecessary to add that England will never so much as hear any *Pourparlers* of a Peace which is not to comprehend His Majesty as Elector.

" I am, etc.,

" HOLDERNESSE."

In a passage quoted from the Memoirs of Baron de Gleichen (THEOSOPHICAL REVIEW, xxii., 45), we have seen with how little ceremony M. de St. Germain was thrown over at the King's Council, and Lord Holdernesse spoke truly when writing :

" What you will say will be authentic ; whereas St. Germain will be disavowed with very little ceremony whenever the Court of France finds it convenient."

The next letter from General Yorke shows that the Duc de Choiseul was working against this much desired peace.

Copy of letter from Major-General Yorke to the Earl of Holderness. Secret.

" *Hague, April 4th,* 1760.

" MY LORD,

" The credit of my political Adventurer, M. de St. Germain, does not seem to have gained ground since my last ; and the Duc de Choiseul seems so much set upon discrediting him that he takes true pains to prevent his meddling in any affairs. I have not seen him since our second interview, and I thought it more prudent to let him alone till he produces something more authentic, comformable to the tenor of the orders I had received ; he is, however, still here.

" The Duc de Choiseul has, however, acquainted M. d'Affry that he should again renew to him peremptorily to meddle in nothing which related to the political affairs of France, and accompanied this order with a menace of the consequence if he did. Madame de Pompadour is not pleased with him neither for insinuating things against

M. d'Affry, of which, either from inclination or apprehension, she has acquainted the Duc de Choiseul. So that he has acquired an enemy more than he had. Marshal Belleisle, too, had wrote to him under M. d'Affry's cover, but in civil terms, thanking him for his zeal and activity, but telling him at the same time, that as the French King had an Ambassador at the Hague in whom he placed his confidence, he might safely communicate to him what he thought was for the service of France ; the tone of Marshal Belleisle's letters shows that he had been more connected with St. Germain than the Duc de Choiseul, who is outrageous against him and seems to have the upper hand.

" In all this correspondence, however, there has appeared as yet nothing about St. Germain and me. The whole relates to the affairs of Holland, the insinuations St. Germain had made of the wrong measures they took here, and the bad hands they were in ; I take it for granted, however, that as the Duc de Choiseul has got the better of him in one instance, he will be able to do it in all the others, especially as in that Minister's letter to M. d'Affry, he desires him to forewarn all the Foreign Ministers from listening to him, as the Court might lose all credit and confidence either about Peace or War, if such a man gained any credit.

" A person of consequence, to whom M. d'Affry showed all the letters, gave me this account, to whom he added, Who knows what he may have said to Mr. Yorke, as I know he has been to wait upon him.   M. d'Affry told this person likewise, that he was fully authorised to receive any proposals from England, and that France having the worst of the quarrel could not make the first proposals ; that he had opened himself to me, as far as could be expected at first, but that as I had taken no notice of him since, they imagined England went back.

" I won't pretend to draw any other conclusion from all this except that they seem still cramped with the unnatural connexion of Vienna which the Duc de Choiseul has still credit enough to support, and consequently, as long as that prevails, we cannot expect anything but chicanes and delays in the negotiations ; they have been repeatedly told that His Majesty cannot and will not treat but in conjunction with his Ally ; the King of Prussia is to be excluded, from whence it is reasonable to conclude that they will try their chance in war once more, tho' Those who govern seem inclined to keep the door open for coming back again if necessary.

" I have the honour to be, etc.,

" JOSEPH YORKE."

In some of this correspondence there are long passages in cipher (numerals), to which there is no key for the public. It is impossible, therefore, to know whether the written words contain the exact meaning or not. Space will not permit the whole correspondence to appear, so we must pass on to a letter from Lord Holdernesse to Mr. Mitchell, the English Envoy in Prussia.

The Earl of Holdernesse. R. 17th May at Meissen (by a Prussian Messenger).[1]

"*Whitehall, May 6th,* 1760.

" Sir,

" You will have learnt by several of my late letters, all that has passed between General Yorke and Count St. Germain at the Hague, and I am persuaded General Yorke will not have failed to inform you as well of the formal disavowal he has met with from M. de Choiseul as of his resolution to come into England in order to avoid the further resentment of the French Minister.

" Accordingly he arrived here some days ago.

[1] This letter from Lord Holdernesse is to Mr. Mitchell, who was the English Representative at the Prussian Court. From this it appears that M. de St. Germain was taken in custody on arriving in England ; and Lord Holdernesse sends word to this effect to the Prussian King. This Baron Knyphausen has been already mentioned as a friend of M. de St. Germain by Mons. Dieudonné Thiébault (Mes Souvenirs de vingt ans de séjour à Berlin, vol. iv., p. 83, 3rd ed., Paris, 1813), who gives an account of their meeting in Berlin at a much later date.

But as it was evident that he was not authorised, even by that part of the French Ministry in whose name he pretended to talk, as his *séjour* here could be of no use, and might be attended by disagreeable consequences, it was thought proper to seize him upon his arrival here. His examination has produced nothing very material. His conduct and language are artful, with an odd mixture which it is difficult to define.

" Upon the whole it has been thought most advisable not to suffer him to remain in England, and he set out accordingly on Saturday morning last with an intention to take shelter in some part of his Prussian Majesty's Dominions, doubting whether he would be safe in Holland. At his earnest and repeated request he saw Baron Knyphausen during his confinement, but none of the King's Servants saw him.

" The King thought it right you should be informed of this transaction ; it is the King's pleasure you should communicate the substance of this letter to his Prussian Majesty.

" I am, with great truth and regard, Sir,

" Your most obedient and humble Servant,

" HOLDERNESSE.

" MR. MITCHELL."

There is a mystery about this visit of M. de St. Germain to England which is not solved by the letter of Lord Holdernesse. Even if he did leave at once, his return must have been almost immediate, since the newspapers and magazines of the period comment on his arrival in May and June, 1760.

In the *London Chronicle*, June 3rd, 1760, there is a long account of his arrival in England, speaking of him in favourable terms. There are hints to be found in various places that he did not really leave ; but so far the actual facts of what occurred are not quite clear. There is more yet to be learned in this curious bye-way of European politics.

Peace appears more difficult to arrange than war, and the personal desires of the French Ministers blocked the way of this mission. Difficult indeed must have been the undertaking for the Comte de St. Germain, thankless the work ; at every turn he met opposition, and could not count on support. All this forms a deeply interesting study, but we must now pass on to the mystical and philosophical side of this little understood life.

CHAPTER VII

MASONIC TRADITION

SONNET PHILOSOPHIQUE
ATTRIBUÉ AU FAMEUX ST. GERMAIN

CURIEUX scrutateur de la nature entière,
J'ai connu du grand tout le principe et la fin.
J'ai vu l'or en puissance au fond de sa minière,
J'ai saisi sa matière et surpris son levain.

J'expliquai par quel art l'âme aux flancs d'une mère,
Fait sa maison, l'emporte, et comment un pépin
Mis contre un grain de blé, sous l'humide poussière,
L'un plante et l'autre cep, sont le pain et le vin.[1]

Rien n'était, Dieu voulut, rien devint quelque chose,
J'en doutais, je cherchai sur quoi l'univers pose,
Rien gardait l'équilibre et servait de soutien.

Enfin, avec le poids de l'éloge et du blâme,
Je pesai l'éternel, il appela mon âme,
Je mourus, j'adorai, je ne savais plus rien.[2]

ONLY a mystic could write, and none but mystics can gauge, words so potent in their meaning, treating as they do of those great mysteries that are unfolded, in their entirety, only to the Initiated. The " Veil of Isis " ever hides the earnest

[1] Referring to occult embryology.
[2] *Poëmes Philosophiques sur l'Homme.* Chez Mercier, Paris, 1795.

student of the Great Science from the vulgarly curious ; hence in approaching the philosophic and mystic side of this mysterious life the difficulties of research become even more complicated by reason of that veil which hides this Initiate from the outer world. Glimpses of knowledge rare among men ; indications of forces unknown to the " general " ; a few earnest students, his pupils, striving their utmost to permeate the material world with their knowledge of the unseen spiritual life ; such are the signs that surround the Comte de St. Germain, the evidences of his connection with that great Centre from which he came. No startling public movement springs up, nothing in which he courts the public gaze as leader, although in many societies his guiding hand may be found.

In modern Freemason literature the effort is made to eliminate his name, and even, in some instances, to assert that he had no real part in the Masonic movement of the last century, and was regarded only as a charlatan by leading Masons. Careful research, however, into the Masonic archives proves this to be untrue ; indeed, the exact contrary can be shown, for M. de St. Germain was one of the selected representatives of the French Masons at their great convention at Paris in 1785. As one account says :
" The Germans who distinguished themselves on

this occasion were Bade, von Dalberg, Forster, Duke Ferdinand of Brunswick, Baron de Gleichen, Russworm, von Wöllner, Lavater, Ludwig Prince of Hesse, Ross-Kampf, Stork, Thaden von Wächter. . . . The French were honourably represented by *St. Germain*, St. Martin, Touzet-Duchanteau, Etteila, Mesmer, Dutrousset, d'Hérecourt, and Cagliostro." [1]

The same category of names, but with more detail, is given by N. Deschamps. [2] We find Deschamps speaking of M. de St. Germain as one of the Templars. An account is also given of the initiation of Cagliostro by the Comte de St. Germain, and the ritual used on this occasion is said to have been that of the Knights Templar. It was in this year also that a group of Jesuits brought the wildest and most disgraceful accusations against M. de St. Germain, M. de St. Martin and many others, accusations of immorality, infidelity, anarchy, etc. The charges were levelled at the Philaletheans, or " Rite des Philalètes ou Chercheurs de la Vérité," founded 1773 in the Masonic Lodge of " Les Amis-Réunis." Prince Karl of Hesse, Savalette de Lange (the Royal Treasurer), the Vicomte de Tavanne, Count de

---

[1] *Magazin der Beweisführer für Verurtheilung des Freimaurer-Ordens*, i., p. 137 ; von Dr. E. E. ECKERT, Leipzig, 1857.

[2] *Les Sociétés Secrètes et la Société, ou Philosophie de l'Histoire Contemporaine*, ii., p. 121. Paris, 1881.

Gebelin, and all the really mystic students of the time were in this Order. The Abbé Barruel [1] indicted the whole body, individually and collectively, in terms so violent and on charges so unfounded that even non-Masons and anti-Mystics protested. He accused M. de St. Germain and his followers of being Jacobins, of fomenting and inciting the Revolution, of atheism and immorality.

These charges were carefully investigated and rejected as worthless by J. J. Mounier, a writer who was neither Mystic nor Mason, but only a lover of honest dealing. Mounier says : " There are accusations so atrocious, that before adopting them a just man must seek the most authentic testimony ; he who fears not to publish them, without being in the position to give decided proofs, should be severely punished by law and, where the law fails, by all right-minded people. Such is the procedure adopted by M. Barruel against a Society that used to meet at Ermenonville after the death of Jean Jacques Rousseau, under the direction of the Charlatan St. Germain." [2]

This view appears to be well corroborated, and

---

[1] *Mémoires sur l'Histoire du Jacobinisme*, ii., p. 554. Paris, 1797.

[2] *De l'Influence attribuée aux Philosophes, aux Franc-maçons et aux Illuminés, sur la Révolution de France*, p. 154. Tübingen, 1801.

is upheld by various writers ; in fact, the proof is conclusive that M. de St. Germain had nothing to do with the Jacobin party as the Abbé Barruel and the Abbé Migne have tried to insist.

Another writer says : " At this time Catholic Lodges were formed in Paris ; their protectors were the Marquises de Girardin and de Bouillé. Several Lodges were held at Ermenonville, the property of the first-named. Their chief aim was ' d'établir une communication entre Dieu et l'homme par le moyen des êtres intermédiaires.' " [1]

Now both the Marquis de Girardin and the Marquis de Bouillé were staunch Royalists and Catholics ; it was the latter, moreover, who aided the unhappy Louis XVI. and his family in their attempted escape. Again, both of these Catholic nobles were personal friends of M. de St. Germain ; hence it hardly appears possible that the assertions of the Abbés Barruel and Migne had any veracious foundation, since the establishing of " Catholic Lodges " certainly does not appear atheistical in tendency, nor the close friendship of true Royalists alarmingly revolutionary. According to the well-known writer Éliphas Lévi,[2] M. de St. Germain was a Catholic in outward religious observance. Although he was the founder of the Order of St. Joachim in Bohemia, he separated himself from

---

[1] *Der Signatstern*, v., art. 19.   Berlin, 1809.
[2] *Histoire de la Haute Magie*, pp. 419, 420.   Paris, 1860.

this society as soon as revolutionary theories began to spread among its members.

Some of the assemblies in which the Comte de St. Germain taught his philosophy were held in the Rue Platrière ; other meetings of the " Philalètes " were held in the Lodge " des Amis-Réunis " in the Rue de la Sourdière.

According to some writers, there was a strong Rosicrucian foundation—from the true Rosicrucian tradition—in this Lodge. It appears that the members were studying the conditions of life on higher planes, just as Theosophists of to-day are doing. Practical occultism and spiritual mysticism were the end and aim of the Philaletheans ; but alas, the karma of France overwhelmed them, and scenes of bloodshed and violence swept them and their peaceful studies away.

A fact that disturbed the enemies of the Comte de St. Germain was the personal devotion of his friends, and that these friends treasured his portrait. In the d'Urfé collection, in 1783, was a picture of the mystic engraved on copper, with the inscription :—

" The Comte de St. Germain, celebrated Alchemist," followed by the words :

" Ainsi que Prométhée, il déroba le feu,
    Par qui le monde existe et par qui tout respire ;
   La nature à sa voix obéit et se meurt.
    S'il n'est pas Dieu lui-même, un Dieu puissant l'inspire."

This copper-plate engraving was dedicated to the Comte de Milly, an intimate friend of M. de St. Germain, a well-known man of the period, and Chevalier de l'Ordre Royal et Militaire de St. Louis, et de l'Aigle Rouge de Braunschweig. This unlucky portrait, however, produced a furious attack from Dr. Biester, the editor of the *Berlinische Monatschrift*, in June, 1785. Amongst some amusing diatribes, the following is worthy of notice, if only to show how inaccurate an angry editor can be. As we have already seen, M. de St. Germain was in the year 1785 chosen representative at the Masonic Conference in Paris. Nevertheless, Herr Dr. Biester, in the *same* year, opens his remarks with the astonishing state-ment : " This adventurer, who died *two years ago* in Danish Holstein " !

Our editor then proceeds to clinch the argu-ment as follows : " I even know that tho' he is dead, many now believe that he is still living, and will soon come forth alive ! Whereas he is dead as a door-nail, probably mouldering and rotting as any ordinary man who cannot work miracles, and whom no prince has ever greeted."

Ignorance alone must excuse our editor from the charge of being a literary Ananias ; but indeed in our own days critics of matters occult are just as ignorant and equally positive as they were a

UBBERGEN

Formerly an old feudal castle at about three-quarters of an hour's distance from Nijmegen; was demolished in 1712 by Count Weldern, its proprietor, who erected on the same spot a new square building.

century ago, no matter what their learning in other respects.

And indeed there was some justification for the statements of Herr Dr. Biester, for a more recent writer says :—

" The church register of Eckernförde shows St. Germain died on February 27th, 1784 in this town in whose church he was entombed quite privately on March 2nd. In the church register we read as follows : " Deceased on February 27th, buried on March 2nd, 1784 the so-called Comte de St. Germain and Weldon—further information not known—privately deposited in this church." In the church accounts it is said : " On March 1st, for the here deceased Comte de St. Germain a tomb in the Nicolai Church here in the burial-place sub N. 1, 30 years time of decay 10 Rthlr. and for opening of the same 2 Rthlr., in all 12 Rthlr." Tradition tells that the landgrave afterwards got St. Germain buried in Slesvig in the Friederiksberg churchyard there in order to consult his ghost in late hours of the night. On the third of April the mayor and the council of Eckernförde gave legal notice concerning his estate. In that it is said : " As the Comte de St. Germain, known abroad, as also here, under the name of Comte de St. Germain and Weldon, who during the last four years has been living in this country, died recently here in Eckernförde, his

effects have been legally sealed, and it has been
found necessary as well to his eventual intestate
heirs, as until now nothing has been ascertained
concerning a left will . . . etc. . . . . Therefore all
creditors are called upon to come forward with
their claims on October 14th." [1]

This passage shows definitely that M. de St.
Germain was well known under the name of
Welldown (it is written in very many different
ways).

But—as to the death—we have much evidence
that he did not die : Madame d'Adhémar says
speaking of M. de St. Germain :—

" He is believed to have deceased in 1784,
at Schleswig, when with the Elector of Hesse-
Cassel ; the Count de Châlons, however, on
returning from his Venetian embassy in *1788*,
told me of his having spoken to the Comte
de Saint-Germain in the Place Saint Marc the
day before he left Venice to go on an embassy
to Portugal. I saw him again on one other
occasion." [2]

And *again from a Masonic* source we get the
following statement :—

" Amongst the Freemasons invited to the great
conference at Wilhelmsbad 15th Feb. 1785 we

[1] Bobé (Louis), *Johan Caspar Lavater's Rejse til Danmark i
Sommeren* 1793, viii., p. 156. Copenhagen, 1898.

[2] Adhémar, *op. cit.*, i., p. 229.

UBBERGEN

find St. Germain included with St. Martin and many others."[1]

And again from a thoroughly Catholic source : the late Librarian of the Great Ambrosiana Library at Milan says :—

" And when, in order to bring about a conciliation between the various sects of the Rosicrucians, the Necromantists, the Cabalists, the Illuminati, the Humanitarians, there was held a great Congress at Wilhelmsbad, then in the Lodge of the " Amici riuniti " there also was Cagliostro, with St. Martin, Mesmer and Saint-Germain."[2]

Evidence there is on both sides, and " Church records " are not always infallible ; how many a *cause célèbre* has arisen from a fictitious death. If the Comte de St. Germain wished to disappear from public life, this was the best way to accomplish his wish.

---

[1] *Freimaurer Brüderschaft in Frankreich*, Latomia, Vol. ii., p. 9.

[2] Cantù Cesare, *Gli Eretici d'Italia*. Turin, 1867, Vol. iii., Disc. lii., p. x, 402.

CHAPTER VIII

Passing now from France to Austria, let us see what Gräffer says in his interesting, though curiously written, sketches. To give, then, a few extracts out of many :

St. Germain and Mesmer

" An unknown man had come on a short visit to Vienna.

" But his sojourn there extended itself.

" His affairs had reference to a far-off time, namely, the twentieth century.

" He had really come to Vienna to see one person only.

" This person was Mesmer, still a very young man.

" Mesmer was struck by the appearance of the stranger. ' You must be the man,' said he, ' whose anonymous letter I received yesterday from the Hague ? '

" ' I am he.'

" ' You wish to speak with me to-day, at this hour, on my ideas concerning magnetism ? '

" ' I wish to do so.'

" ' It was the man who has just left me, who in a fatherly way has guided my ideas in this channel. He is the celebrated astronomer Hell." [1]

" ' I know it.'

" ' My fundamental ideas, however, are still chaotic ; who can give me light ? '

" ' I can do so.'

" ' You would make me happy, sir.'

" ' I have to do so.'

" The stranger motioned Mesmer to lock the door.

" They sat down.

" The kernel of their conversation centred round the theory of obtaining the elements of the elixir of life by the employment of magnetism in a series of permutations.

" The conference lasted three hours. . . .

" They arranged a further meeting in Paris. Then they parted." [2]

That St. Germain and Mesmer were connected in the mystical work of the last century we know from other sources,[3] and that they again met and worked together in Paris, is verified by

---

[1] Maximilian Hell (Imperial Court Astronomer). To this highly respected scholar are due thanks for having given the impulse to take up magnetism scientifically and practically. See *Oesterr. National Encyclopädie*, art. " Mesmer."

[2] *Kleine Wiener Memoiren*, i., 81. Wien, 1846.

[3] H. P. BLAVATSKY, *Theos. Gloss.*, p. 214. London, 1892.

research among the records of the Lodge meetings already mentioned. This meeting in Vienna must have taken place before Mesmer began his work in Paris judging by the context. Vienna was the great centre for the Rosicrucians and other allied Societies, such as the " Asiatische Brüder," the " Ritter des Lichts," etc. The former were the largest body who really occupied themselves deeply with alchemical researches and had their laboratory in the Landstrasse, behind the Hospital. Among them we find a group of St. Germain's followers.

To quote Franz Gräffer again :—

" One day the report was spread that the Comte de St. Germain, the most enigmatical of all incomprehensibles, was in Vienna. An electric shock passed through all who knew his name. Our Adept circle was thrilled through and through : St. Germain was in Vienna ! . . .

" Barely had Gräffer [his brother Rudolph] recovered from the surprising news, than he flies to Hiniberg, his country seat, where he has his papers. Among these is to be found a letter of recommendation from Casanova, the genial adventurer whom he got to know in Amsterdam, addressed to St. Germain.

" He hurries back to his house of business; there he is informed by the clerk : ' An hour ago a gentleman has been here whose appearance has astonished us all. This gentleman was neither tall nor short, his build was strikingly proportionate, everything about him had the stamp of nobility. . . . . He said in French, as it were to himself, not troubling about anyone's presence, the words : " I live in Fedalhofe, the room in which Leibnitz lodged in 1713." We were about to speak, when he was already gone. This last hour we have been, as you see, sir, petrified.' . . . .

" In five minutes Fedalhofe is reached. Leibnitz's room is empty. Nobody knows when ' the American gentleman ' will return home. As to luggage, nothing is to be seen but a small iron chest. It is almost dinner time. But who would think of dining ! Gräffer is mechanically urged to go and find Baron Linden ; he finds him at the ' Ente.' They drive to the Landstrasse, whither a certain something, an obscure presentiment, impels them to drive post haste.

" The laboratory is unlocked ; a simultaneous cry of astonishment escapes both ; at a table is seated St. Germain, calmly reading a folio, which is a work of Paracelsus. They stand dumb at the threshold ; the mysterious intruder slowly closes the book, and slowly rises. Well know the two perplexed men that this apparition can be no other in the world than the man of wonders. The description of the clerk was as a shadow against a reality. It was as if a bright splendour enveloped his whole form. Dignity and sovereignty declared themselves. The men were speechless. The Count steps forward to meet them ; they enter. In measured tones, without formality, but in an indescribably ringing tenor, charming the innermost soul, he says in French to Gräffer : ' You have a letter of introduction from Herr von Seingalt ; but it is not needed. This gentleman is Baron Linden. I knew that you would both be here at this moment. You have another letter for me from Brühl. But the painter is not to be saved ; his lung is gone, he will die July 8th, 1805. A man who is still a child called Buonaparte will be indirectly to blame. And now, gentlemen, I know of your doings ; can I be of any service to you ? Speak.' But speech was not possible.

" Linden laid a small table, took confectionery from a cupboard in the wall, placed it before him and went into the cellar.

" The Count signs to Gräffer to sit down, seats himself and says : ' I knew your friend Linden would retire, he was compelled. I will serve you alone. I know you through Angelo Soliman, to whom I was able to render service in Africa. If Linden comes I will send him away again.' Gräffer recovered himself ; he was, however, too overwhelmed to respond more than with the words : ' I understand you : I have a presentiment.'

" Meanwhile Linden returns and places two bottles on the table. St. Germain smiles thereat with an indescribable dignity. Linden offers him refreshment. The Count's smile increases to a laugh. ' I ask you,' said he, ' is there any soul on this earth who has ever seen me eat or drink ? ' He points to the bottles and remarks : ' This Tokay is not direct from Hungary. It comes from my friend Katherine of Russia. She was so well pleased with the sick man's paintings of the engagement at Mödling, that she sent a cask of the same.' Gräffer and Linden were astounded ; the wine had been bought from Casanova.

" The Count asked for writing materials ; Linden brought them. The ' Wundermann ' cuts from a sheet of paper two quarters of the sheet, places them quite close to each other, and seizes a pen with either hand simultaneously. He writes with both, half a page, signs alike, and says : ' You collect autographs, sir ; choose one of these sheets, it is a matter of indifference which ; the content is the same.' ' No, it is magic,' exclaim both friends, 'stroke for stroke, both handwritings agree, no trace of difference, unheard of ! '

" The writer smiles ; places both sheets on one another ; holds them up against the window-pane ; it seems as if there were only one writing to be seen, so exactly is one the facsimile of the other ; they appear as if they were impressions from the same copper-plate. The witnesses were struck dumb.

" The Count then said : ' One of these sheets I wish delivered to Angelo as quickly as possible. In a quarter of an hour he is going out with Prince Lichtenstein ; the bearer will receive a little box. . . .'

" St. Germain then gradually passed into a solemn mood. For a few seconds he became rigid as a statue, his eyes, which were always expressive beyond words, became dull and colourless. Presently, however, his whole being became re-animated. He made a movement with his hand as if in signal of his departure, then said : ' I am leaving (*ich scheide*) ; do not visit me. Once again will you see me. To-morrow night I am off ; I am much needed in Constantinople ; then in England, there to prepare two inventions which you will have in the next century—trains and steamboats. These will be needed in Germany. The seasons will gradually change—first the spring, then the summer. It is the gradual cessation of time itself, as the announcement of the end of the cycle. I see it all ; astrologers and meteorologists know nothing, believe me ; one needs to have studied in the Pyramids as I have studied. Towards the end of this century I shall disappear out of Europe, and betake myself to the region of the Himalayas. I will rest ; I must rest. Exactly in eighty-five years will people again set eyes on me. Farewell, I love you.' After these solemnly uttered words, the Count repeated the sign with his hand. The two adepts, overpowered by the force of such unprecedented impressions, left the room in a condition of complete stupefaction. In the same moment there fell a sudden heavy shower, accompanied by a peal of thunder. Instinctively they return to the laboratory for shelter. They open the door. St. Germain is no more there. . . .

"Here," continues Gräffer, "my story ends. It is from memory throughout. A peculiar irresistible feeling has compelled me to set down these transactions in writing once more, after so long a time, just to-day, June 15th, 1843.

"Further, I make this remark, that these events have not been hitherto reported. So herewith do I take my leave." [1]

The curious character of Franz Gräffer's sketches is striking. From other sources it can be learned that both of these Gräffers were personal

---

[1] *Op. cit.*, ii., pp. 136–162. It is to be regretted that Gräffer's florid account opens the door to a slight suspicion of charlatanry in the mind of the modern student of occultism. It is probably, however, his way of looking at the matter which is at fault. A more experienced student would probably have described the interview far otherwise, although he might have testified as strongly to precisely the same facts.

friends of St. Germain, both were also Rosicrucians. And though no date is given of the interview here recorded, we can deduce it approximately from another article in the same volume, where it is said : " St. Germain was in the year '88, or '89, or '90, in Vienna, where we had the never-to-be-forgotten honour of meeting him." [1]

That the Comte de St. Germain was also a Rosicrucian there is no doubt. Constantly, in the Masonic and Mystic literature of the last century the evidences are found of his intimacy with the prominent Rosicrucians in Hungary and Austria. This mystic body originally sprang up in the central European States ; it has, at various times and through different organisations, spread the Sacred Science and Knowledge with which some of its Heads were entrusted—the same message from the one Great Lodge which guides the spiritual evolution of the human race. Traces of this teaching, as given by our mystic, are clearly found, and are quoted by Madame Blavatsky, who mentions a " Cypher Rosicrucian Manuscript " [2] as being in his possession. She emphasises also the entirely Eastern tone of the views held by M. de St. Germain.

The fact that M. de St. Germain possessed this rare work shows the position held by him. Turning

[1] *Op. cit.*, iii., p. 89.
[2] *The Secret Doctrine*, ii., p. 212, 3rd ed.

again to *The Secret Doctrine*,[1] we find his teaching on " Numbers " and their values, and this important passage links him again with the Pythagorean School, whose tenets were purely Eastern. Such passages are of deep interest to the student, for they prove the unity which underlies all the outward diversity of the many societies working under different names, yet with so much in common. On the surface it would appear that better results might have been attained had all these small bodies been welded into one large Society. But in studying the history of the eighteenth century, the reason is evident. In Austria, Italy and France, the Jesuits were all-powerful and crushed out any body of people who showed signs of occult knowledge. Germany was at war, England also at war ; any large masses of students would certainly have been suspected of political designs. The various small organizations were safer, and it is evident that M. de St. Germain went from one society to another, guiding and teaching ; of his constant connection with the Masonic circles we have other proofs ; M. Björnstahl writes in his book of travels :—

" We were guests at the court of the Prince-Hereditary Wilhelm von Hessen-Cassel (brother of Karl von Hessen) at Hanau, near Frankfort.

[1] ii., pp. 616, 617.

" As we returned on the 21st of May 1774 to the Castle of Hanau, we found there Lord Cavendish and the Comte de St. Germain ; they had come from Lausanne, and were travelling to Cassel and Berlin.

" We had made the acquaintance of these gentlemen in Lausanne at the house of Broglio."[1]

This is a most interesting statement, for it shows also the continued intercourse of M. de St. Germain with the Bentinck family, with whom he had so much intercourse in 1760 at the Hague.

A Masonic friend [2] sends me the following information and extracts of letters, drawn from Masonic sources in the Royal Library in Wolfen-büttel. He says :—

" With this post I send you a photo of the letter from Count de Welldone to the Duke Friedrich August of Braunschweig, nephew of Ferdinand of Braunschweig, and also from Frederick II. of Prussia, his uncle.

" Dr. K. Weber in ' From four Centuries ' writes, vol. I., p. 317 :—

" ' In October 1776 he came to Leipzig as v. Welldone, where he offered many secrets for the use of the Town Council, that he had

---

[1] BJÖRNSTAHL, J. J. *Reise in Europa in* 1774, vol. v., pp. 229, 237.

[2] LANGVELD, L. A.—The Hague.

gathered together during his travels in Egypt and Asia.'

" The letter from Welldone is in the Wolfenbüttel Library (not in the Archives). There I found various other remarkable letters. All are from and to Freemasons. Among others one from Dubosc, Chamberlain in Leipzig, who on the 15th of March 1777 wrote to Fr. August of Braunschweig :—

" ' After a mysterious stay, the actual St. Germain, known at the time under the name of Comte Wethlone (Welldone), who took great care to give us to understand that he hid under this name his true quality of Prince Rákoczy, took a fancy to associate with me.'

" From the minister v. Wurmb (Dresden) on the 19th of May 1777 from Dresden :—

" ' I employed the fortnight I spent in Leipzig to feel the pulse of the famous St. Germain who at the present time has taken the name of Comte de Woeldone and besides, at my request he came here to stay some time. I found him between 60 and 70 years old.' "

The original letter of M. de St. Germain has been photographed and the translation is as follows written from Leipzig : it has already been shown that by the Church Records he had a right to this name and was known and acknowledged as Comte de Welldone.

" Monseigneur,

" Will your Highness kindly permit me that I open my heart to you ; I am hurt that the Councillor, Mr. du Bosc, used means which could not be agreeable to me, to make me known the Orders You have entrusted him with, according to what he says in his letter, and which surely could by no means concern me ; the Baron de Wurmb, as well as the Baron de Bishopswerder will always be honourable witnesses of the rectitude and uprightness of the step I have taken, which was rendered necessary by the respect and the zealous and faithful attachment which I have dedicated to you for my whole life, Monseigneur ; the delicacy enjoined me at first to say nothing about my motive.

" I will hasten as much as possible to carry out the affairs both important and indispensable for the locality I am in, in order that I may immediately afterwards have the inexpressible joy of paying my court to you, the best of Princes ; when I shall have the honour of being well known to you, Monseigneur, I expect with full certitude from your fine discernment all that justice which is due to me and which will be extremely appreciated by me, coming from your part.

" I am, in duty bound,

" Your respectful, faithful and humble servant

" LE C. DE WELLDONE.

" *Leipzig, May 8th,* 1777."

Monseigneur

Votre Altesse veut bien permettre que
je lui ouvre mon cœur. Il est ulcéré depuis
que M. le Conseiller da Bose s'est servi d'une
manière qui ne pouvoit pas n'être agreable
pour me signifier les ordres dont Elle
l'avoit honoré, a ce qu'il dit dans sa lettre
et qui surement ne pouvoient me regarder
en aucune manière; Mr le Baron de
Wurmb, ainsi que Mr le Baron de Bisch-
opswerde seront toujours d'honorables
temoignages de la bonté et droiture de
ma demarche que le respect et l'attachement zelé, et fidele que je vous ai voué
pour la vie Monseigneur, m'ont absolument rendu necessaire quoique ma
Delicatesse m'eut d'abord enjoint de
ne rien dire du motif —

Count de Welldone (Comte de St. Germain) to F. A

Je presserai autant que possible de terminer
des affaires aussi importantes qu'indispensa
:bles au lieu ou je me trouve pour avoir
tout aussitot après l'inexprimable joië
d'aller vous faire ma cour Prince incompa:
:rable, quand j'aurai l'honneur de vous etre
bien connu, Monseigneur, je me promet.
bien surement de votre justice et par
Discernement toute celle que on me doit,
et que venant de votre part me sera
extremement chere, je suis comme
mon devoir, mon inclination et mon
attachement respectueux, et fidele

De Votre Altesse Ser^{me}

Monseigneur

Leipzig ce 8 mars 1777

Le trèshumble et trèsobeissant serviteur
C. de Welldone

schweig in Berlin, General in the Prussian service.

More evidence of this visit is found in a letter from the Saxon Minister von Wurmb, who was himself an earnest Mason and a Rosicrucian.

"Correspondence of the Prior El, with the Minister Wurmb, o.d. Fr. a Sepulcro,

"*Gimmern, June 3rd, 1777.*

"The 'a Cygne tr' (Gugomos) has most certainly not gone to Cyprus, but to England. . . . M. de St. Germain chiefly on my account has come to Dresden. If he does not disguise himself in an extraordinary manner, then he will not suit us, altho' he is a very wise man." [1]

Evidently a visit was expected which had to be disguised ; this gives a clue to the reason why M. de St. Germain was travelling in Leipzig and Dresden under that name of Comte Weldon. According to Cadet de Gassicourt, he was travelling member for the " Templars," going from Lodge to Lodge to establish communication between them. M. de St. Germain is said [2] to have done this work for the Paris Chapter of the " Knights Templar." Investigation proves him to have been connected with the " Asiatische Brüder," or the " Knights of St. John the Evangelist from the East in Europe," also with the

[1] *Der Signatstern, oder die enthüllten sämmtlichen sieben Grade der mystischen Freimaurerei*, iii., pt. 1. Berlin, 1804.

[2] CADET DE GASSICOURT, *Le Tombeau de Jacques de Molay*, p. 34. Paris, 1795.

" Ritter des Lichts," or " Knights of Light," and with various other Rosicrucian bodies in Austria and Hungary ; and also with the " Martinists " in Paris.

He founded, according to Éliphas Lévi, the Order of St. Joachim, but this statement is not supported by any historical evidence at present forthcoming, though many of his students and friends were members of this body. Everywhere, in every Order where real mystic teaching is to be found, can we trace the influence of this mysterious teacher. A letter of his to the Graf Görtz at Weimar is quoted, saying that he had " promised a visit to Hanau to meet the Landgraf Karl at his brother's house in order to work out with him the system of ' Strict Observance '—the regeneration of the Order of Freemasons in the aristocratic mind—for which you also so earnestly interest yourself."

A summarised account from the " Gartenlaube " [1] fits in here ; the letters are said to be authentic ; and from internal evidence there is little doubt about it ; for the information has to do with the Masonic work on which the Comte de St. Germain was engaged :—

" Karl-August went to the Landgrave Adolf von Hessen-Philippsthal-Barchfeld. St. Germain was there and was duly presented to the Duke,

---

[1] *Brause Jahre Bilder* in Gartenlaube, 1884, n. 38, 39.

was charming in conversation and the latter asked, after supper, his host about the count.

" ' How old is he ? '

" ' We do not know anything sure about it. It is a fact that the count knows details which only contemporains could tell in the same way. It is fashion now in Cassel to listen respectfully to his stories and to be astonished about nothing. The count does not praise himself, neither is he an importune talk-teller, he is a man of good society, whom every one is glad to have. He is not much liked by the head of our house, Landgraf Frederick II., who calls him a tiresome moralist. But he is in connection with many remarkable men and has an extraordinary influence upon others. My cousin, Landgrave Karl of Hesse, is much attached to him, they work together in Freemasonry and other dark sciences. Lavater sends him chosen men. He can speak in different voices and from different distances, can copy any hand he sees once, perfectly—he is said to be in connection with spirits who obey him, he is physician and geognost and is reported to have means to lengthen life.'

.   .   .   .   .

" The Duke went to Görtz, whom he knew well to be an enemy and opponent of Goethe. Therefore in this moment of excitement he took the part of the marshal.

" Görtz received the rare visit in a submissive way ; when from slight hints he could notice that the duke was not desirous to speak about Goethe, his countenance was still more brightened.

" ' At the beginning of May, dear Marshal, I made a highly interesting acquaintance at the Landgraves in Barchfeld,' said finally the duke, not without embarrassment. ' An acquaintance which I wish to keep up. It was a certain Comte Saint Germain, who is staying at Cassel ; please write to this gentleman and invite him courteously to come over here.'

" Görtz promised to meet this request within the shortest time and to the best of his ability.

" When the duke had gone away, he sat down to his writing table and wrote as follows :

" Letter of Count Görtz :—

" ' Triumph, dear count. Your knowledge of men, your addresses conquer. You have foretold well : our gracious master is enchanted with you and asks you hereby, in due form through me to come to his court.

" ' You are really a wonder-worker, for his detested, plebeian favourite now totters . . . a little help, one stroke of your genius and the advocate of Frankfurt, who intrudes upon us, is checkmated. Will you fight him openly now, or do you prefer to make first an incognito personal survey of the territory ? put down one or two mines for him and show yourself only when he is totally beaten out of the field ? and then take his place with far more right and power ?

" ' I leave all this to your sagacity. Rely upon me as before, entirely, and a small *élite* of faithful aristocrats, one or two of which you may wish to bind closer to you if you think it good.

" ' Always yours truly '

" ' Count Görtz, marshal of court.'

" St. Germain's answer :

" ' Dear Count !

" ' I am quite ready to associate further with you and your companions in opinion, very grateful for the complaisant invitation. I will follow it later on.

" ' In the present moment I have promised to visit Hanau, to meet the Landgrave Karl at his brother's and work out with him the system of the " Strict Observance "—the regeneration of the order of freemasons in an aristocratic sense— which interests you too so much.

" ' The Landgrave is to me a dear and sympathetic protector, and if not a prince regnant, his position in Schleswig attached to Danish service, is very princely. I will, by all means, before I decide quite for the Landgrave, come to Weimar, liberate you from the hated intruder, and recognise the field there. Maybe I will prefer to do incognito at first.

" ' Recommend me faithfully to your master, and promise my visit for some time to come.

" ' In the name of prudence, silence and wisdom I salute you

" ' Yours

" St. Germain.' "

From internal evidence this is an authentic letter, for the Comte de St. Germain would certainly have been helping in this body, based as it was on the old " Order of the Temple " which will be treated at length later on. It was, moreover, to save themselves from persecution that these members called themselves " Free and Adopted Masons," and adopted the signs and words of Masonry. Undoubtedly the " Strict Observance " sprang from the most secret " Order of the Temple," a truly occult organisation in the olden time.

At the suggestion of the Comte de St. Martin and M. Willermoz the name was changed because of the suspicions of the police ; the new one chosen was " The Beneficent Knights of the Holy City."

Baron von Hund was the first Grand-Master ; on his death the general leadership was vested in the Grand Duke of Brunswick, an intimate friend of M. de St. Germain. All these various organisations will be dealt with in order ; at present they are merely mentioned to show the connecting link formed by M. de St. Germain between the separate bodies, with whom M. de St. Germain had work to do ; an Austrian writer in a recent article says :—

" In the Masonic and Rosicrucian literature one often finds hints as to the relations of St. Germain to the secret societies of Austria. One of St. Germain's adherents in Vienna was Count J. F. von Kufstein, in whose Lodge (in the house of Prince Auersberg) magical meetings were held which generally lasted from 11 p.m. to 6 a.m. St. Germain was present at one such meeting and expressed his satisfaction with the workings.

" . . . St. Germain collected old pictures and portraits ; he was addicted to alchemy, believed in universal medicine and made studies as to animal magnetism. He impressed people, especially the higher classes, by his French manners, his wide knowledge and his talkativeness. This ' Bohemian ' so much attacked by historians, played the part of a political agent during the peace negotiations between France and Austria. Again, he is said to have distinguished himself in the year 1792 in the revolution.

" He was the ' Obermohr ' of many mystic brotherhoods, where he was worshipped as a superior being and where every one believed in his ' sudden ' appearances and equally ' sudden ' disappearances. He belongs to the picture of ' Old Vienna ' with its social mysteriousness ; where it was swarming with Rosicrucians, Asiatics, Illuminates, Alchemists, Magnetopaths, Thaumaturgs, Templars, who all of them had many and willing adherents.

" Dr. Mesmer who knew the Comte St. Germain well from his stay in Paris, requested him to come to Vienna in order that he might pursue his study of animal magnetism with him. St. Germain stayed secretly here and was then known as the ' American of the Felderhof ' which latter became later on ' Laszia House ' in the Lugeck N. 3. Dr. Mesmer was much helped by the Count and here in Vienna his (Mesmer's) teaching was written down. Soon Mesmer gained followers but he was obliged to leave the town. He went to Paris where his ' Harmonious Society '—a secret society of savants—continued to exist. In Vienna St. Germain came in touch with many mystagogues. He visited the famous laboratory of the Rosicrucians in the Landstrasse behind the hospital where he instructed for some time his brethren in the sciences of Solomon. The Landstrasse, situated on the outskirts of Vienna, was for many centuries a region of spooks.

" Below in the Erdberg the Templars and the estates of their order and outside town in the Simmering there was in the times of Rudolf II. the gold kitchen where the eccentric fraternity endeavoured to make gold. It is certain that the Comte de St. Germain has been in Vienna in the year 1735, and also later. The arrival of the Count (who enjoyed at that time a great prestige) at once created a great sensation in the initiated circles." [1]

The following is a list of some of the societies, more or less connected with Masonry, which had " Unknown Heads." Translated they are as follows :

The Canons of the Holy Sepulchre.

The Canons of the Holy Temple of Jerusalem.

The Beneficent Knights of the Holy City.

The Clergy of Nicosia in the Island of Cyprus. [2]

The Clergy of Auvergne.

The Knights of Providence.

The Asiatic Brothers ; Knights of St. John the Evangelist.

The Knights of Light.

The African Brothers.

Then there are groups of various Rosicrucian bodies widely spread in Hungary and Bohemia.

[1] MAILLY, A. de—Der Zirkel, March 1st, 1908.

[2] This is the Society mentioned by the Minister Wurmb in the letter quoted.

In all of these bodies enumerated can be traced clearly the guiding hand of that " messenger " of the eighteenth century, or of some of his immediate friends and followers. Again in all of these groups can be found, more or less clearly, those fundamental principles which all the true messengers of the Great Lodge are bound to teach : such, for instance, as the evolution of the spiritual nature of man ; reincarnation ; the hidden powers of nature ; purity of life ; nobleness of ideal ; the Divine power that is behind all and guides all. These are the clues which show without possibility of doubt to those who search for truth, that Lodge whence came the Comte de St. Germain, the messenger whose life is here but roughly sketched.

His work was to lead a portion of the eighteenth century humanity to that same goal which now, at the end of the nineteenth century, again stands clear before the eyes of some Theosophists. From his message many turned away in scorn, and from the present leaders the blind ones will to-day turn away also in scorn. But the few whose eyes are opening to the glad light of a spiritual knowledge, look back to him who bore the burden in the last century with gratitude profound.

APPENDICES

APPENDIX I

DOCUMENTS CONCERNING THE APARTMENT IN CHAMBORD
OFFERED TO THE COMTE DE SAINT GERMAIN BY
LOUIS XV. (1758).

NATIONAL RECORD OFFICE.
BOX—OLD REGIME—BLOIS AND CHAMBORD (WORKS)
1747—1760, O'.—1326.

*Letter from M. Collet, Manager of the Castles of Chambord
and of Blois, to the Marquis de Marigny,
Director general of the Buildings.*

"Chambord, May 10th, 1758.

" Sir,

" I take advantage of the opportunity kindly offered
me by the Comte de St. Germain to accompany him to
Paris in order to make some arrangements concerning
him as well as to transact some business which must be
finished by the end of next week. I hope that during
those few days you will allow me to wait upon you. . . ."

M. de Marigny to M. Collet.

"Marigny, May 19th, 1758.

" Sir,

" I willingly give you permission to profit by the opportunity you have in accompanying the Comte de St.
Germain to come to Paris and stay here. . . ."

M. Collet to the Marquis de Marigny.

" Chambord, Dec. 4th, 1758.

" Sir,

" . . . the Comte de St. Germain arrived at Chambord on Saturday last with two gentlemen.   He will stay for five or six days and then goes to Paris, having the kindness to take me with him.   I hope as soon as I arrive to have the honour, Sir. . . ."

M. Collet to the Marquis de Marigny.

" Chambord, May 8th, 1758.

" Sir,

" . . . the Comte de St. Germain arrived here on Saturday last, this being his second visit to Chambord : I had two rooms prepared for some of his people as well as three more with kitchens and offices on the ground floor for his accommodation.   I have had no alterations made in this part of the Castle but only urgent repairs."

The Abbé de la Pagerie to M. de Marigny.

" Blois, Aug. 12th, 1758.

" Sir,

" Not being fortunate enough to live sufficiently near to you to pay my respects, I make up for it by writing in order that I may recall myself to your memory.   I am most grateful for the civilities with which you have honoured me which will ever remain dear in my memory. I fully appreciate them and none can be more devoted to you than myself.

" I often see M. Begon who has the honour to be known to you, he is quite engrossed in his building operations which are very fine.   M. de St. Germain who arouses the curiosity of the whole country is constantly expected : I have met him twice at dinner parties.   He seems to

be a man of great knowledge and guided by principle.
. . . Poor M. de Saumery, the Governor of Chambord cannot last much longer, his leg is in a terrible state. . . ."

Answer of M. de Marigny to the Abbé de la Pagerie.

" Versailles, Sept. 2nd, 1758.

" I have received, Sir, the letter of the 12th inst. which
you did me the honour of writing to me. It is a fact
that the King has granted to M. de St. Germain lodgings
in the Castle of Chambord, and you are right in saying
that he is a man of worth. I had the opportunity
of convincing myself of the fact in various interviews
which I have had with him, and real benefits are to be
derived from his superior knowledge. . . ."

The following correspondence took place with regard to some
dwellings round the Castle of Chambord.

*M. de Saumery, Governor of the Castle, to the Marquis
de Marigny.*

" Paris, April 15th, 1759.

" . . . I consider that these out-houses will do as
lodgings for the use of the workmen that the Comte de
St. Germain will bring here for the establishment of his
Manufactory."

(On April 5th, 1759, an order had been given that the said
outhouses were to be rented for the benefit of the King, it
therefore does not seem that M. de St. Germain had the use of
them.)

The Marquis de Marigny to the Comte de St. Florentin.

" Versailles, Sept. 8th, 1760.

" Sir,

" I have the honour to inform you of an affair which
took place in the Court of Chambord Castle at half past

ten p.m. on the 26th ult., the principal actor in it being Sieur Barberet (or Barberes), who is lodging there in the service of M. de St. Germain. This latter has spent the year in Holland and went from thence to England. . . ."

(It was an attempt by this man to stab M. Collet with his sword.)

The Comte de St. Florentin to the Marquis de Marigny.

" Versailles, Sept. 15th, 1760.

" I am writing to M. de Saumery, Governor of Chambord, to know why Sieur Barberes who is in the service of M. de St. Germain remains in the Castle ? "

(The Sieur de Barberes appears to have tried to reserve for his own use two gardens to which he had no title. M. de Saumery seems to have secretly supported him in opposition to M. Collet.)

M. Collet to the Marquis de Marigny.

(Still with regard to the Barberes affair.)

" Chambord, June 16th, 1760.

" The Sieur Barberes is still here. He is causing his followers to spread a report that M. de St. Germain is in Paris and may be here within the fortnight, and that what has been said about him will not be forgotten and that the Gazette has purposely said what it has. . . ."

APPENDIX II

CORRESPONDENCE BETWEEN THE DUC DE CHOISEUL AND
THE COMTE D'AFFRY WITH REGARD TO THE COMTE
DE ST. GERMAIN, FROM THE ARCHIVES IN PARIS.

RECORD-OFFICE OF FOREIGN AFFAIRS (PARIS).
HOLLAND

No. 557.   Folio 153.

The Hague, Feb. 22nd, 1760.

(Received Feb. 26th, answered March 10th.)

" Your Grace

" M. d'Astier writes to say that there is at Amsterdam
a certain Comte St. Germain whom I believe once spent
a long time in England and who affects many pecu-
liarities.

" He speaks in an extraordinary way of our finances
and of our Ministry, and affects to be entrusted with an
important Mission with respect to the financial position
of the Country. . . ."   D'AFFRY.

D'Affry to the Duc de Choiseul.—In cipher.

No. 562.   Folio 200.

STATE RECORD OFFICE, THE HAGUE.

March 7th, 1760.

" People who came here from Amsterdam for the
festivities (the wedding of Princess Caroline with the
Prince of Nassau-Dillenburg) as well as a letter from

M. D'Astier which I received to-day, go to prove that
M. de St. Germain continues to make the most extraordinary assertions in that town."

No. 563.   Folio 212–214.

The Hague, March 10th, 1760.

    " M. le Duc.

    " M. le Comte de St. Germain came here to see me the
day before yesterday ; he held much the same language
to me as I was told that he held in Amsterdam.   He has
just left my house and his conversation has been on the
same subject : he told me in the first place that he could
not give me a sad enough picture of the state of our
finances : that he entertained a certain scheme (the
marriage of the Princess Clementine Caroline) for recruit-
ing them, and, in a word, that he would save the kingdom.   I let him say as much as he would, and when he
left off talking I asked him if the Controller General
knew of his scheme.   He said ' no ' and he took the
opportunity of telling me much evil of the predecessor
of M. Bertin.   He seemed to me to be especially
inimical to Messrs. Paris de Montmartel and Du Verney.
He told me that he was closely connected with M. the
Maréchal de Belleisle and he showed me two letters
from him that he has received since he came to Holland,
in which M. de Belleisle speaks graciously to him of the
ardour of his zeal, but they contained mere generalities
and no particulars.

    " I confessed to M. de St. Germain that I did not
altogether understand his scheme, and he owned on his
side that he explained it badly and said he would bring
me the plan of it to-morrow.   I asked him what his
journey to Holland had to do with this scheme ; he did

not answer me very clearly to the point, but told me that his object in general was to secure the credit of the principal bankers there for us.

"I shall have the honour of reporting to you next Friday, M. le Duc, what M. de St. Germain may have said and communicated during the day, to-morrow. I do not know whether all that he gives out is founded on the most exact truth, but he certainly holds very extraordinary notions."

March 11th.

"M. de St. Germain has communicated to me his scheme, which is known and even recommended by M. Bertin. I will send you a report next Friday of our conversation on this matter. . . ." D'AFFRY.

No. 564. Folio 217.

The Hague, March 14th, 1760.

(Received March 18th. Answered the 20th.)

"M. le Duc,

"I have seen the scheme of which M. de St. Germain had informed me. I have sent it back to him, and I shall take the first opportunity of telling him that affairs of this kind have nothing to do with the Ministry with which I am honoured. I could not meddle with them unless so commanded, and desired to exert myself to find credit for His Majesty's funds in Amsterdam or in other towns in Holland. I think I have discovered the cause of M. de St. Germain's antipathy towards Messrs. Paris de Montmartel and Du Verney, in article 11 or 12 of the draft of the Edict, which states that there will be a ' cash account.' As this article struck me on first reading it, I remarked to M. de St. Germain that this ' cash ' might prove an immense treasure to those who

managed it. He replied briskly that if Messrs. Paris
were allowed to become masters of it, they would soon
become so of the whole finances of the kingdom, and that
he had come to Holland solely to complete the formation
of a Company adequate to the responsibility of this
Fund ; in which case I think he would be annoyed to see
it pass into other hands than those of his associates, if
this scheme were adopted.

" M. de St. Germain told me that M. Bentinck de
Rhoone had complained to him of my reserve towards
him, and that I never spoke to him on matters of business. He added that M. Bentinck had assured him that
no-one was less English than himself, that he was a true
Patriot and more French than I believed. I replied to
M. de St. Germain with general common-places, so as to
make him feel, however, that I thought it strange that
M. de Bentinck should have given him this commission,
and still more strange that he should have undertaken it.
I have considered it my duty to report to you all that has
taken place between this man and myself."   D'AFFRY.

Folio 239.

Versailles, March 19th, 1760.

" Sir,

" I send you a letter from M. de St. Germain to the
Marquise de Pompadour which in itself will suffice to
expose the absurdity of the personage ; he is an adventurer of the first order, who is moreover, so far as I
have seen, exceedingly foolish. I beg you immediately
on receiving my letter to summon him to your house,
and to tell him from me that I do not know how the
King's Minister in charge of the Finance Depart. will look
on his conduct with regard to this object, but that—as
to myself—you are ordered to warn him that if I learn

that far or near, in much or little, he chooses to meddle with Politics, I assure him that I shall obtain an order from the King that on his return to France he shall be placed for the rest of his days in an underground dungeon !

" You will add that he may be quite sure that these intentions of mine concerning him are as sincere as they will surely be executed, if he give me the opportunity of keeping my word.

" After this declaration you will request him never again to set foot in your house, and it will be well for you to make public and known to all the foreign Ministers, as well as to the Bankers of Amsterdam, the compliment that you have been commanded to pay to this insufferable adventurer."

Folio 215.

Letter from the Comte de St. Germain
to the Marquise de Pompadour.

March 11th, 1760.

" Madame,

" My pure and sincere affection for the welfare of your esteemed Nation and for yourself, not only are unchanged in whatever part of Europe I may be, but I will not remain there without making it apparent to you in all its purity, sincerity and strength.

" I am just now at the Hague, staying with M. le Comte de Bentinck, Seigneur of Rhoone, with whom I am closely connected. I have been so successful that I do not think France has any friend more judicious, sincere and steadfast. Be assured of this, Madame, *whatever you may hear to the contrary*.

" This gentleman is all-powerful here as well as in England, a great Statesman and a perfectly honest man.

He is absolutely frank with me. I have spoken to him of the charming Marquise de Pompadour from the fulness of a heart whose sentiments towards you, Madame, have long been known to you and are surely worthy of the kindness of heart and the beauty of soul which have given rise to them. He was so charmed with them that he is quite enraptured : in a word, you may rely on him as on myself.

" I think with good reason that the King may expect great services from him, considering his power, his uprightness and sincerity. If the King thinks that my relations with him can be of any help, I will not spare my zeal in any way for his service, and my voluntary and disinterested attachment to his sacred person must be known to him. You know the loyalty that I have sworn to you, Madame : command, and you shall be obeyed. You can give Peace to Europe without the tediousness and the difficulties of a Congress ; your commands will reach me in perfect safety if you address them to the care of M. le Comte de Rhoone at the Hague, or if you think better, to the care of Messrs. Thomas and Adrian Hope, with whom I reside at Amsterdam. What I have the honour of writing to you appears to me so interesting, that I should greatly reproach myself if I kept silence on it towards you, Madame, from whom I have never hidden and will never hide anything. If you have not time to reply to me yourself, I entreat you to do so thro' some safe and trustworthy person ; but do not lose a moment, I implore you, by all the affection, all the love you bear to the best and worthiest of Kings. . . .

" P.S. I entreat you, Madame, to be so good as to interest yourself in the trial about the capture of the ' Ackermann,' the most unjust and scandalous that has ever occurred at sea : I have an interest in it amounting to fifty thousand crowns, and Messrs. Emery and Co. of Dunkirk are commissioned to demand restitution of the vessel. I beg of you once more to have justice done to me by the Royal Council, to which this iniquitous case is shortly to be referred. You will kindly remember that you promised last summer not to allow injustice to be done to us."

No. 567.   Folio 245.
                    The Hague, March 21st, 1760.
    (Answered 31st by M. d'Affry.)

        " M. le Duc,
    " The Comte Rhoone de Bentinck has not only informed me through M. de St. Germain, but has also caused me to be told by other persons, how much he wished to be associated with me and in the most urgent way ; I replied that not having had hitherto any connection with him, it appeared to me useless to begin it, that I should nevertheless be always ready to form one with persons who, as good Dutch patriots, would feel it well for their country to cultivate the friendship and good-will of His Majesty ; that I knew that he (M. de Bentinck) had always cast aside those principles, so desirable for his Country and for himself, and that his conversion in this respect would require proofs lasting longer than he would care to attempt ; he was informed of my reply, and was not discouraged by it.

    " I felt bound to inform the Pensionary, M. de Selingulande (?) and the Comte de Hompesch. They told me that M. de Bentinck only desired to approach us in order to renew his credit here and in England, where it is ever falling, and that he probably wished to be nominated one of the Plenipotentiaries at the future Congress of the Republic. . . ."

Folio 285.

Versailles, March 31st, 1760.

" M. le Comte d'Affry,

" On the report, Mons., that I made to the King regarding the indirect steps that M. le Comte de Bentinck has taken in order to induce you to enter into some special negociations with him, His Majesty commands me to inform you, that his desire is, that you should confine yourself, as you have hitherto done, with respect to M. de Bentinck, within the limits of becoming courtesy. . . ."

No. 573.   Folio 294.

The Hague, April 3rd, 1760.

" M. le Duc,

" . . . I have reason to believe that M. de Bentinck, no longer seeing M. de St. Germain coming to my house, and knowing that I have openly discredited him, is ready to disavow him, and to say that he only continues to see this adventurer because he is a kind of fool who amuses him, but the Republican Chiefs know that M. de Rhoone too well not to be aware that he would have taken advantage, and eagerly, of the proposals that the fellow has taken upon himself to make him, if they had been accepted."   D'AFFRY.

No. 576.   Folio 304.

The Hague, April 5th, 1760.

(Answd. 11th.   No. 207.)

" M. le Duc,

" I reply to-day to the letter that you did me the honour to write me on the 19th of last month concerning M. le Comte de St. Germain.   I have not been able to do so earlier, because the indiscreet conduct (to say no more) of this adventurer seemed to me to require thorough investigation before reporting it to you, but this conduct is such, that I consider it my duty to bring it to the cognisance of His Majesty.

" The day after the receipt of your letter, M. de St. Germain, who had arrived from Amsterdam, came to see me.   He came with the Chevalier de Bruhl and M. de Kauderbach, and told me that those gentlemen were going to take him to see the Comte de Goloffkin at Riswick, where I was also to go.   I said to M. de St. Germain that I wished to speak to him before he left, and I told him at once the substance of what you had written to me about his scheme.   He was overwhelmed by it, and I ended my conversation with him by requesting him to come to my house at 10 o'c. the following morning.   The next moment I imparted to M. de Kauderbach the contents of your letter, which determined him at once not to take M. de St. Germain to Riswick.

" M. de St. Germain did not come to my house, and as I believed that what I had very clearly explained to him would be enough to make him prudent, and even to determine him to leave the country, I did not consider that I ought to urge him to come to my house again, and that it was enough to have communicated here what you had written to me, to the chief Ministers of the Republic and to some Foreign Ministers, and to have written to M. d'Astier at Amsterdam to warn the principal Bankers to be on their guard against the proposals that M. de St. Germain might make to them.

" M. d'Astier has informed me that Messrs. Thomas and Adrian Hope among others were greatly annoyed and embarrassed at having had him to stay with them,

and that they would take the first possible opportunity
to get rid of him, but the two packets that you were
so good as to forward to me from M. le Maréchal de
Belleisle, appeared to me to show that this man was not
keeping to the instructions I had given him, and that he
might involve us in fresh difficulties. I received these
letters on Tuesday. I sent to M. de St. Germain to come
to my house on the Wednesady morning ; he did not
come, and the day before yesterday, Thursday, M. de
Brunswick, in the presence of Messrs. Goloffkin and de
Reischach, and after having communicated to him our
counter-declarations, told me he had learnt that His
Majesty had been so good as to order the letters to be sent
to me that M. de St. Germain had written to Versailles,
and that I should probably soon receive others, since he
knew that M. de St. Germain had written some very
lengthy ones since I had forbidden him my house, but
that he had positively refused to see him ; that he had
nevertheless learnt that he had seen others than himself,
and that the fellow was still hatching plots here ! That
if not accused of anything, still he was a very dangerous
character in our times and place and that a man of such
effrontery might embarrass and retard a negociation by a
single step. I then thought I ought to speak, and I told
Prince Louis that I was fully authorised to declare to
him and to Messrs. de Goloffkin and de Reischach that M.
de St. Germain was a man absolutely disavowed by us
and that no trust or confidence should be placed in anything he might choose to say about our affairs or our
Government. I said further to M. de Brunswick that
when he had an opportunity, perhaps that very day, of
seeing Mr. Yorke, I begged him earnestly to make the
same declaration to him for me. I also made it yesterday
morning to the Pensionary and the Registrar.

" On my return from Riswick the evening before last, I sent to request M. de St. Germain to pay me a visit. He was not found at home : I sent him a card of invitation to come to me here yesterday morning at eight o'c. I was obliged to send again to find him, and he came at last. I did not think I ought to pass on to him the letters of M. Belleisle, for fear of the bad use he might make of them, but I told him that M. le Maréchal had told me by the express order of the king that I was to listen to all he had to say to me. I asked him if there were overtures relating to our soldiery, and he said ' no.' I asked him if they concerned our Navy or our finances. And again he said ' no,' to which I replied that they could only be political, and thereupon I read him all that you wrote me as to the fate that awaits him if he returns to France. At first he affected great indifference, then he expressed astonishment at the treatment with which such a man as himself was threatened, but he seemed to me to be at last troubled by it. Since, however, he did not appear to me resolved to abandon the schemes which his disquietude suggests, I warned him very seriously again, as we parted, that if he chose to meddle in any way whatever with His Majesty's affairs and interests, I should report it to you, and I should say publicly here, that all that he had put forward was absolutely repudiated by His Majesty and by His Ministry. I went at once to keep my appointment with Mr. Yorke, after having dismissed the matter which I reported to you in my despatch under No. 575. I asked Mr. Yorke if M. de St. Germain had been at his house. He told me that he had been there twice ; that on the first visit he had spoken to him of the Peace, and that he had replied merely with generalities about the sincere desire of England to see an end of the War ; he said that on the second visit, he, Mr. Yorke, had become more reserved because he then knew that my house had been forbidden to M. de St. Germain. He added that the Duke of Newcastle had written to him with reference to the report he had given of this man's first visit, that he might tell him in reply that overtures of peace on the part of France would always be welcomed in London, thro' whatever channel they might come, but I do not know whether Mr. Yorke communicated this reply to him.

" I beg of you, M. le Duc, to communicate this despatch to M. le Maréchal de Belleisle and I am very sure that he will cease all correspondence with a man whose conduct is such as I have described to you. I add here a packet for M. de Belleisle by private express, in which I return him with my letter the two letters which he had sent me for M. de St. Germain.

" I ought to tell you further that M. de St. Germain has the assurance to assert everywhere, and even to tell *me* that his Majesty has been so good as to grant him Chambord, on the same terms as granted to the late M. le Maréchal de Saxe, excepting the revenues . . . which he said he should not have wished to have." D'AFFRY.

No. 578.   Folio 312.

The Hague, April 8th, 1760.

(Recd. 12th.   Answd. 24th.   No. 209.)

" M. le Duc,

" I was informed yesterday that altho' M. de St. Germain continued to see M. de Bentinck de Rhoone, I might rest assured that M. de St. Germain had said that I could not do otherwise than carry out your wishes ; that he knew you did not like him, but that if you had

a place in His Majesty's Council, he also had the same !
I replied that assertions so absurd could mislead no one,
and that I should consider it derogatory to my Ministry
to contradict them. This information was given to me
by one of the Republican Chiefs who in fact is an enemy
of M. de Bentinck, but whom I have always known as an
honourable man.

" M. de St. Germain is absolutely discredited, and he
will meet with no credence here from any Foreign
Minister or Minister of the Republic ; but I considered it
my duty to make you acquainted with all this, because
this man may give false impressions and such as would be
disadvantageous to us, as to a pretended division in our
Ministry, which does not exist. . . ." D'AFFRY.

No. 206.

Versailles, April 11th, 1760.

" To M. le Comte d'Affry.

" I will reply first, Monsr., to the letters that you have
done me the honour to write me on the 3rd instant as
to the different objects of the Despatches which formed
the correspondence which was forwarded to you by my
last courier. . . .

" You have seen, Monsr., by the special letter that I
had the honour of writing to you about M. de St. Germain the opinion that I held as to this insufferable adventurer ; I assure you that every one of His Majesty's
Ministers holds the same opinion as myself, and the King
has commanded me to tell you expressly not only to discredit in the most humiliating and most emphatic manner
by your words and by your actions, this so-called Comte
de St. Germain, among all those whom you may suspect
of knowing this rascal throughout the whole Dominion

of the United Provinces, but His Majesty further desires that through the friendliness of the States General towards him, you may arrange that they should have this fellow arrested, so that he could be transported to France and punished in accordance with the heinousness of his offence. It is to the interest of all Sovereigns and of Public Faith that this kind of insolence should be put down, which with no authority, chooses to meddle with the affairs of such a Power as France. I think that the case in question should be regarded as at least as much ' privileged ' as those which usually demand the recla-mation and extradition of a malefactor. Thus the King has reason to hope that on your statement, this M. de St. Germain will be arrested and conducted under safe escort to Lille.

" I confess that I have thought you very lenient to-wards him, and that I perhaps should not have been prudent enough to refrain from ordering him a good sound drubbing after the last conversation that you had with him.

" What he told you about Chambord is an imposture of the highest degree. In short, Monsr., the King abso-lutely wills that this adventurer shall be cried down and disgraced in the United Provinces, and that he shall if possible be punished as his attempt deserves. His Majesty has strictly charged me to desire you by his authority to give this matter your best attention.

" P. S. Would it not be possible, besides the request to the States General for the arrest of this St. Germain to have an article inserted in the Dutch Gazette which would set down this rascal once for all ? And be an example to all impostors who may wish to imitate him ? The King furthermore, has approved of this course and you will carry it out in full, if you consider it possible."

No. 581.   Folio 357.

The Hague, April 17th, 1760.

(Answd. 24th.   No. 2091—M. le Comte d'Affry.)

" M. le Duc,

" I have thought it my duty to delay till to-day returning the express that you sent me, that I might report
to you more fully the way in which I have tried to carry
out the orders of His Majesty regarding the so-called
Comte de St. Germain.   Yesterday, I visited the Pensionary, to whom I read all that you have done me the
honour to write to me concerning this rash adventurer,
and I demanded from him the arrest and extradition in
the name of His Majesty.

" He appeared embarrassed by it, but nevertheless
promised me to do all that depended on him in the
matter.

" The Duke of Brunswick told me that he could not
appear in it, but that he would meet us in all that might
facilitate it, and that I well knew how much he himself
desired that such a fellow should be unmasked.

" The Registrar told me that he did not doubt that
this man would be given up to us, but that as M. de
Bentinck is the Head of the Committee of Rade (?) and
this affair must be considered there, during the absence
of the States of Holland, I feared instantly that the
escape of M. de St. Germain would be facilitated, and
what I feared has happened.

" I expected news of this affair yesterday morning
when M. de Kauderbach came to see me.   He asked me if
I knew of the departure of M. de St. Germain.   I told him
I did not ; he informed me that the evening before last,
between 7 and 8 o'c., M. de Bentinck had been to the
house of this adventurer, that he had left it again before

9 o'c., that then M. Pieck de Zoelen had come there, that he did not stay very long, that afterwards M. de Bentinck had come again between 9 and 10, and that he had remained there until after midnight ; that M. de St. Germain had gone to bed, and that at 5 o'c. in the morning he had taken his tea, and that a lackey of M. de Bentinck's had appeared at the door with a hired carriage and four, into which this rascal stepped, but the landlord could not tell what road he had taken, nor could he say if M. de Bentinck's lackey went with him.

" This departure was so hasty that he left at the house of the landlord his sword and his belt and a packet of " coepeaux " (?) either silver or tin, and some bottle of some unknown liqueur. I controlled myself enough to conceal from M. de Kauderbach the indignation that I felt at the conduct of M. de Bentinck. I said nothing to him as to my orders about the reclamation and extradition. I simply asked if he were certain of all the particulars that he had just given me. He told me that he had them from M. de St. Germain's landlord himself, who was a Saxon. He suggested sending him to me. We sent for him ; he came, and confirmed all that M. de Kauderbach had told me.

" When M. de Kauderbach had left my house, I sent to request the Pensionary to let me see him ; he had only returned home from a grand dinner at which he had been present at 7 o'c. and he put off my visit until this morning at 9 o'c. I went to him and asked him what about the affair of M. de St. Germain. He replied that he alone could not take the responsibility on himself, that it was quite necessary that I should present a memorial to M. de Bentinck, President of the Committee of Rade ; that he thought that this Tribunal would decide on the arrest of M. de St. Germain, but not on his extradition before being authorised so to do by the States of Holland at their approaching Convocation. I replied that I should certainly not present a memorial to M. de Bentinck, and that I would tell him why. I then told him the particulars of M. de St. Germain's departure, and of what preceded it, excepting the circumstances which might compromise the host, and I told him these details in a way to make him believe that I had discovered the comings and goings of M. de Bentinck in the house, and the appearance of his hired lackeys with the carriage, only thro' the careful watching of my spies. He seemed to me to be honestly indignant at all that he heard. I said that since the escape of the adventurer had been furthered by the Hague, he had perhaps sought refuge at Amsterdam, and that I was going to write to our Commissary of Marine, M. d'Astier, to request that this scoundrel be arrested in the name of His Majesty, and detained under safe guard until I received final orders. In fact I wrote him the letter of which I now append a copy. I then told the Pensionary that as the adventurer might take refuge in some other Province of the States General, I should at once request His Majesty's permission to present a public Petition to their High Mightinesses, and that if the Province of Holland in particular, or any other, should refuse this act of justice or seek to evade it by furthering the escape of M. de St. Germain, we should know very well where to find him again and that I felt sure, whether he were found in England or elsewhere he would be given up to us directly Peace was declared. This last seemed to me to embarrass the Pensionary greatly, and I should not be surprised if he were arrested at Amsterdam on our requisition, but I am persuaded that he will not be there, and that he will have already gained the frontier of the Republic. The Memorial which I request your permission to present to the States General, and of which I here append the rough draft, may appear, if His Majesty approves of it, in all the Gazettes, and will cast a stigma on this adventurer from which he can never recover. It is a kind of injudicial condemnation, which will brand him throughout Europe.

" I believe the rascal to be sorely pressed for money. He has borrowed from the Jew ' Boas ' two thousand florins for which he has deposited with the Jew three opals, real or false, in a sealed paper. The two thousand florins should be repaid on the 25th inst. and Boas told M. de Kauderbach yesterday that if the letter of exchange for the money did not arrive on the 25th, he should put up these opals for public sale. I shall act with regard to M. de Bentinck as you desired me in your last despatch, unless His Majesty should give me fresh orders in this respect, and if I meet him one of these days I shall speak to him of M. de St. Germain and his departure, without committing myself, but so as to force him to disavow his conduct altogether, and his connection with this adventurer." D'AFFRY.

Folio 384.

*Letter from M. le Comte d'Affry, of April 17th, 1760,
to M. d'Astier at Amsterdam.*

" The so-called Comte de St. Germain, Monsr., whom you saw at Amsterdam and who has been sent here from thence, is an adventurer and impostor.

" He has had the impudence, without any authority or commission from His Majesty or His Ministry, to busy himself with working and negociating about the most important interests of His Majesty and of the Kingdom.

" After my report of this to the King, and after the letters which he himself wrote to Versailles, His Majesty issued orders to me for the reclamation of this impudent impostor and that I should demand his extradition, to be sent to us.

" As he suddenly left The Hague yesterday morning, and he may perhaps be at Amsterdam, I authorise you in this case, and command you in His Majesty's name, at once to demand from the Magistracy of Amsterdam the arrest of this impostor and his detention in sure and safe custody until we have agreed on the method of transporting him to the Austrian Netherlands, to be taken thence to the first of our fortifications.

" I here append a letter for Messrs. Horneca (?) and Co. in which I request them to be security for you in the expenses that this commission may require, for which you will answer in my name and under the guarantee of these gentlemen."

Rough draft of memorial to be presented to the States General for the exposure of the so-called Comte de St. Germain and to demand his arrest and extradition.

" High and Mighty Lords,

" An unknown person who styles himself the Comte de St. Germain and to whom the King, my master, graciously granted an asylum in his kingdom, has abused it.

" He came some time ago to Holland, and recently to The Hague, where, without authority from His Majesty or His Ministry, and without any commission, this indiscreet fellow chose to announce that he was authorised to discuss the affairs of His Majesty. The King, my master, gives me express orders to make this known to your High Mightinesses, and *publicly*, so that no-one throughout your dominions may be deceived by such an impostor. His Majesty further authorises me to proclaim this adventurer as a man without authorisation, who has taken advantage of the asylum granted him by the Prime Minister to meddle with the government of the Country, with as much impropriety as ignorance, and falsely and boldly declaring that he was authorised to treat of the most essential interests of the King, my master.

" His Majesty does not doubt that your High Mightinesses will do him the justice that he has the right to expect from your friendship and equity, and that you will give orders that the so-called ' Comte de St. Germain ' be arrested and taken under safe escort to Antwerp, to be sent from thence to France.

" I hope that your High Mightinesses will grant me this request without delay."

No. 209.   Folio 377.

Versailles, April 24th, 1760.
                To M. d' Affry,
" I have received, Monsr., all the letters that you have done me the honour to write to me, and of which the last, No. 582 (581?), is of the 18th inst.

" The King approves, Msr., of your presenting to the States General the Memorial of which you have sent me the draft, concerning the so-called Comte de St. Germain. . . ."

No. 584.

Recd. 29th (Answered May 1st).

The Hague, April 25th, 1760.
                " M. le Duc,
" It is believed that the so-called Comte de St. Germain is gone to England ; I am even told that the fear of being arrested disturbed him so much that he did not

dare to remain in the town of Helvoetsluys (?) and had taken refuge at once on board a Packet boat, on which he remained up to the moment of his departure, without choosing to set foot on land. Others believe that he made for Utrecht, whence he must have reached Germany.

" The line of conduct that M. Bentinck de Rhoone has maintained with this adventurer is now notorious, and still further lessens his credit in all classes of the State.

" One of the chief Republicans has given me the translation which I here append of a passage from the second volume of the history of the Country, which has just appeared. You will see from it, M., that an attempt is made to unmask M. de Bentinck, not only to those who compose the Government but also in the Bourgeois class and among the people, by means of a Dutch book which is generally read in the Seven Provinces. The indecency with which he strove to make himself agreeable to the people at the time of the Revolution is a thing that we could never forget." D'AFFRY.

No. 585. Folio 388.

The Hague, April 27th, 1760.

(Ansd. May 10th, M. d'Affry.)

" M. le Duc,

" A Professor of mathematics at the University of Leyden, named Alaman, and who is the man most closely connected in this country with M. Bentinck de Rhoone, came to see me yesterday under the pretext of repeating the invitation that he once gave me to go and dine with him and to see the collections of machinery and of Natural History of which he has the care, but he really only visited me to speak about M. de Bentinck.

" He began by asking me if I knew of a man named Lignières who called himself a gentleman of Franche Comté, and who had come here accompanied by a Swiss, named Vivet, to introduce a machine for hollowing the beds of rivers and cleaning the canals.   I replied that this man had been to see me, that I had asked him if, as a subject of the King, he had offered this machine to our Ministry before taking it to foreigners ; that Lignières had told me that he *had* performed this duty, but that the machine had not been accepted ; that I did not think much of it from what Lignières told me and from what I knew of forcing methods and their friction.   I added that what gave me the worst opinion of this undertaking was the protection given to its promoters by the Comte de St. Germain, who had recommended them to me. Alaman told me that he was very glad to have the opportunity of gaining information as to everything concerning this celebrated man, if I would kindly give it to him.   I replied that I would conceal nothing from him, and I then gave him the whole history of this adventurer since his arrival in Holland, assuring him that I was convinced that M. de Bentinck would altogether disavow what such an impostor had put forth in his name.   Upon that I gave him a detailed account of all the impostures that the adventurer had practised here.   He seemed surprised at it, and I did not conceal from him how much surprised I was myself at the conduct of M. de Bentinck up to the moment of the adventurer's escape. M. Alaman made but a poor defence for him on that point, and then leaving M. de St. Germain, he spoke of M. de Bentinck exactly as M. de St. Germain had done, telling me among other things that M. de Bentinck throughout his conduct, had no other object than the interests and the welfare of the country ; that my estrangement with regard to him was merely because I knew him only from the reports of his enemies, and that if I would take means to become personally acquainted with him I should soon give up my prejudices against him. I replied, that at the beginning of my residence here I had endeavoured to make M· de Bentinck's acquaintance, and this is the simple truth, but that he had always refused the advances I had made, and I owned that they did not continue long, because I soon saw that he did not respond to them.

" I said further that M. de Bentinck's behaviour on the departure of M. de St. Germain from the Hague did not appear to me to show any sign of the desire he suggested to oblige us. M. Alaman replied that he did not know what had occurred as to that, but that he could assure me that M. Bentinck had a real desire to know me. I replied coldly that he might assure him that I should always be glad to show him the courtesy due to a man of his rank and occupying one of the highest posts in the Republic.

" If M. de Bentinck continues the desire to approach us, I shall behave towards him outwardly as His Majesty commands me, but in such a way, that the Republicans cannot take umbrage at it and that M. de Bentinck cannot take advantage of it in any way.

" This new departure of his, coming from a man who has been uniformly devoted to him for the last twenty years, convinces me that the so-called Comte de St. Germain had really spoken in his name, since he had acted very much like Alaman.

" M. de Bentinck has always openly opposed us, and with so much bitterness that it is impossible to believe that the wish to oblige us should make him renounce his principles in order to further our interests, and I am strongly of opinion that all he is doing to approach us is merely owing to his great desire and need to maintain and increase his credit here.

" He must feel that the surest way of raising it would be to get into close relations with the principal foreign Ministers, who may be charged with endeavouring to promote Peace, and I think that on the contrary it is most essential that instructions should be issued here that M. de Bentinck should never have any trust placed in him by us. I even consider it necessary in the last place, that M. Grimaldi should be informed of the conduct of M. de Bentinck and of the report that I have given of it to you, before he leaves Paris to come here."
D'AFFRY.

No. 586.   Folio 399.

The Hague, April 29th, 1760.

(Recd. May 3rd.—Ansd. May 10th, No. 212—M. d'Affry.)

" . . . The westerly winds detained the English Mail Boat at Helvoet till the 20th. Easterly and north-easterly winds followed, so that the last letters received from London are of the 21st. We shall be unable to receive news from England until these latter winds have ceased.

" I have received the letters that you did me the honour to write to me the 24th of this month. I shall have the honour of replying to them by Friday next.

" I will take the opportunity of presenting to the States General the Memorial concerning the so-called Comte de St. Germain." D'AFFRY.

(Here ends the first volume 4 (?) (1760.)

No. 221.   Folio 3.

(Here begins the 2nd volume—May–August.)

The Duc de Choiseul to M. d'Affry.

Versailles, May 1st, 1760.

" I have received, Monsr., the letters that you did me the honour to write to me on the 21st, 22nd, and 25th, of last month. . . . I doubt the so-called Comte de St. Germain having gone to England. He is too well known there to have any hope of taking people in."

No. 587.   Folio 5.

The Hague, May 2nd, 1760.

(Ansd. 10th, No. 202, M. le Cte. d'Affry.)

" M. le Duc,

" I now reply to the two letters with which you have honoured me, of the 24th of last month, under Nos. 207 and 209. Yesterday morning I carried out His Majesty's orders in delivering to the President of the (week ?) the Memorial of which I here append copy. This Memorial has been taken ad referendum by all the Provinces, under the pretext that M. de St. Germain being no longer here, it was enough that each Province should be informed of His Majesty's demand, in case this adventurer should reappear in any of the Provinces. It seems to me that this is really sufficient, as this fellow is no longer here, and as the publication of my Memorial in the gazettes discredits him everywhere, and for ever ; wherefore I shall let the matter drop, if His Majesty sends me no fresh orders on the subject.

" The wind has varied since the day before yesterday, but it has returned to the point of the north-east ; so that we have still no news from England. . . ." D'AFFRY.

Folio 8.

Memorial presented by M. d'Affry to the States General in order to unmask the so-called Comte de St. Germain, and to reclaim him in the name of the King.

" An unknown person who goes by the name of the ' Comte de St. Germain,' and to whom the King, my master, has generously given shelter in His Kingdom, has abused this favour.

" He came some time ago to Holland, and recently to The Hague, where, without authority from His Majesty or His Ministry, and without any commission, the impudent fellow took it into his head to announce that he was authorised to negociate in the affairs of His Majesty.

" The King, my master, expressly commands me to make this known to your High Mightinesses, and publicly, so that no-one throughout your dominions may be taken in by this impostor.

" His Majesty further commands me to reclaim this adventurer as an unauthorised man who has abused in the highest degree the shelter given to him, by meddling with and discussing the Government of the Kingdom, with as much impropriety as ignorance, and by falsely and boldly asserting that he was authorised to treat on the most important interests of the King, my master.

" His Majesty does not doubt that your High Mightinesses will administer the justice that He has a right to expect from your friendship and equity, and that you will give orders for the arrest of the so-called Comte de St. Germain and his removal under safe escort to Antwerp, to be taken thence to France.

" I hope that your High Mightinesses will grant me this request without delay."

Issued at the Hague, April 30th, 1760.

Signed—L. C. D'AFFRY.

No. 588.   Folio 11.

The Hague, May 5th, 1760.

" Monsr. le Duc,

" . . . I have appealed to the Pensionary, I have requested him to clear away this difficulty—[it is a question of guns and ammunition sent from Sweden to Amsterdam]. He has not ventured to undertake it, and has constantly declared to me that it was necessary that I should present a Memorial to the Committee of Rade, and that I should send it to M. de Bentinck who is at the head of it. The Registrar told me the same thing, and I had gone to the latter Minister in order to know what had happened relative to the Memorial that I had presented against the so-called Comte de St. Germain. M. de Bentinck came to join me ; I took this opportunity of saying before him, all that I thought of this adventurer : I even said that he had compromised *him* in his letters, and that I was fully persuaded that it was unauthorised by him, but I said nothing to him of what I knew he had done to countenance the man before his departure. M. de Bentinck made no reply and remained greatly embarrassed. I then spoke of the Memorial that I had to send to him, and nothing could be better than the way he talked of that. I went to see him the next day ; he received me in his grand apartment, and gave me the most cordial welcome. He told me that what I demanded would not raise the slightest difficulty, and in fact I received that very day the order from the Committee of Rade not only for permitting the passage of our

Artillery, but also for the immediate return of the money deposited at the different bureaux.

" M. de Bentinck has affected to assist us on this occasion as promptly as we could well desire, but we can only attribute this to its being to his interest to appear on good terms with us ; but I shall never swerve from the line of conduct that His Majesty has deigned to indicate to me regarding him." D'AFFRY.

No. 590.   Folio 17.

The Duc de Choiseul to the Comte d'Affry.

Versailles, May 10th, 1760.

" I have received, Monsieur, all the letters that you have done me the honour of writing to me (Nos. 585, 586, 587), the last of which have been forwarded to me by the express that you sent me on the 5th inst. and which I return to you without delay. M. de Bentinck does not deserve that we should trouble ourselves very much about him. We have long known how far to trust his designs, and some very equivocal demonstrations of repentance will not undo twenty years of odious and improper proceedings on his part, relating to France. . . .

" I have already seen in some gazettes your Memorial on the so-called Comte de St. Germain ; I will have it inserted also in that of France, and this publication will at least in part accomplish our object regarding this adventurer. . . ."

No. 593.   Folio 37.

The Hague, May 12th, 1760.

" M. le Duc,

" . . . M. de Galitzin also informs me that the so-called Comte de St. Germain, on reaching England, found a State messenger who prohibited him going further, and who had orders to re-embark him on the first vessel that sailed. He has probably returned to Helvoet, but it is clear that he would not have lost a moment in leaving the territory of the Republic. I will however speak to the Pensionary about it this very day. M. de Galitzin adds that the English Minister would not allow the Comte de St. Germain to be in London, because he believed that we only affected to be displeased with him in order to give him a pretext for going there and more assured means of serving us there; but the Memorial which I have published can leave no further suspicion as to this." D'AFFRY.

No. 595.   Folio 45.

The Hague, May 14th, 1760.

" M. le Duc,

" Yesterday afternoon I saw M. Yorke; I dictated to him what was underlined in your despatch. . . .

" . . . Before we parted I asked M. d'Yorke the history of the so-called Comte de St. Germain. He told me that this adventurer had not been arrested at Harwich, but that he had been so on reaching London, under an order from Mr. Pitt, and that a head clerk of this Minister had been to question him; that the evidence of this head clerk showed that the Comte de St. Germain had seemed to him a sort of lunatic, in whom, however, he discovered no evil intent. On this report the Minister desired this adventurer to be told that having here and elsewhere given proofs of his incautiousness, it was not fitting that he should be permitted to be in London, nor in England, and consequently he has been reconducted to Harwich. He returned to Helvoetsluis and went on immediately to Utrecht, and from thence to Germany. M. d'Yorke thinks that he will go to Berlin, or join His

Prussian Majesty.   I asked him if it was true that this proceeding on the part of this adventurer had really been caused by the distrust of the English Minister.   He replied that he was entirely ignorant of the motive, but that he had informed his Ministry that he had no doubt that it was from a wish to oblige us."   D'AFFRY.

Folio 142.

The Hague, June 27th, 1761.

" M. le Duc,

" A man who calls himself a gentleman of Franche Comté who bears the name of Linières, and who seems formerly to have called himself ' Montigni,' came here some years ago, about the same time as the so-called Comte de St. Germain : they had formed a society, in which, however, St. Germain did not appear publicly, for the construction of hydraulic machines suitable for cleansing Ports, Canals and Rivers.   They had issued shares in order to provide funds for this undertaking. During this time Linières came to tell me that he had offered the machinery to our Ministry, but that M. de Bellidor who had examined it, had told him that it could be accepted only by Commissioners nominated by our ' Academy of Sciences ' ;   that he, Linières, not being able to entrust his secret to so many persons, had decided to come here to offer his machine, with the certainty of thus being able to preserve his secret intact.   I thought it my duty to put some questions to him, in order to see if this machine could really be of much use to us in the clearing of our ports or of our rivers, but his replies were so uncertain and showed so little capacity that I found he did not know even the first principles of mechanics. He undertook and carried out the construction of this machine in the town of Woorbourg, near here, and he invited me some months ago, to go there to see it tested, which did not prove successful. . . . [here follows a description of the machine].

"There is a second one which has succeeded better. It is a pump which has much less friction than ordinary pumps, but I believe it is the same as that which has been used at Besançon for several years.

"M. de Linières, convinced that these machines are of great use, has begged me to allow him the honour of writing to you about them and of sending you the papers which he sent me on the subject, and which I here append. You will find in them a request to the King, a scheme of privilege, a memorial of observation concerning these inventions ; a translation of an extract from the resolutions of the States of Holland respecting these machines and lastly an account of the products of the machine of (?) in order to compare them with the results of M. de Linières' new machine ; but this last paper contains nothing but a calculation, which is absolutely false on consideration and after the experiment which I witnessed and which has not been verified since. M. de Linières is settled at Vienne, and if you think it worth while to send any answer to what I have the honour of telling you, I will communicate it to him as soon as your reply reaches me. . . ."   D'AFFRY.

No. 793.   Folio 299.

The Hague, March 23rd, 1762.
The Comte d'Affry to the Duc de Choiseul.
(no cipher).

"Monsieur,

" . . . The so-called Comte de St. Germain who came here two years ago, who gave out that he was entrusted with full powers to negociate a treaty between us and England, and with regard to whom I received orders to reclaim him as an impostor, has since then strayed into the Provinces of the Republic and their environs, under borrowed names, and carefully concealing himself ; but within the last few days I have learnt that under the name of an Amsterdam merchant, named Noblet, he has purchased an estate in Guelders, called Huberg, which was sold by M. le Comte de Weldern and on which, however, he has not yet paid more than about thirty thousand francs in French money. I have thought it my duty to inform you of this fact, and to ask you if it is His Majesty's wish that I should take proceedings against this man by a fresh Memorial to the States General against him, or if His Majesty considers that I had better let him alone, since the principal object of my actions has been gained by discrediting him in such wise that he has not ventured to show himself since, and he is reduced to trying to make dupes of people with his chemical secrets to gain a living." D'AFFRY.

No. 311.   Folio 327.

Versailles, April 10th, 1762.

The Duc de Choiseul to M. d'Affry.

(no cipher).

" . . . We have punished the so-called Comte de St. Germain for the insolence and imposture of his attempt, and we must leave to this adventurer the task of completing the general discredit into which we have plunged him. . . ."

No. 506.   Folio 54.

The Minister of Foreign Affairs to M. d'Affry.

No. 245.   Versailles, Jan. 25th, 1761.

" . . . The article you noticed in the Brussels Gazette of the 12th practically does for the Count of St. Germain or the adventurer who bears his name, and it is a blunder on the part of the manager of the Paper in the absence of the Editor who is at the moment in Paris.

" What especially struck me was the fact that the Editor of the Gazette has been correctly informed as to the message you received from the Maréchal de Belle-Isle with regard to the Comte de St. Germain. . . ."

APPENDIX III

FROM THE PAPERS OF SIEUR BENTINCK VAN RHOON, IN THE ARCHIVES OF THE PALACE OF H. M. THE QUEEN OF HOLLAND, TRANSLATED FROM THE DUTCH.

Sunday, March 9th, 1760.

He (St. Germain) told me . . . that there would be no obstacles on the part of England to the Peace, that the obstacles would come from France . . . that the King of France and Mme de Pompadour, the whole Court as well as the whole of the country, were passionately longing for Peace ; that one man alone prevented it, viz. the Duc de Choiseul, won over as he was by the Court of Vienna (the Queen of Hungary) . . . that all the confusion and misfortunes in Europe were due to the Treaty of Versailles in 1756 . . . in which there was a secret clause giving the Flanders to the Infante, in exchange for Silesia, which latter had to be subdued, given up, and made over to the Queen of Hungary. . . . There was but one way to get out of it, and that was by concluding Peace between England and France ; that the usual methods of " Preliminaries, Congresses, and Conferences " would mean spinning out things indefinitely and would cause War again, the mere idea of which makes one shudder ; he was of opinion that if only some possible propositions were brought forward, or if only some honest men in whom people could put faith would intervene, Peace would be made . . . it being as

necessary to England as it was to France; that the King
and Mme de Pompadour wished it fervently, that the
King of England wished it not less, that the Duke of
Newcastle and Count Granville (Charles Foronshead)
were very much in favour of it (speaking of Chesterfield,
he said firmly while looking fixedly at me to see what I
would answer : " Chesterfield is a mere trifler "), that
Pitt who now made common cause with the two others,
had always crossed him hitherto, but that Pitt was hated
by the King . . . that a Scotchman of the name of
Crammon who lived in Paris had received a letter from
Neuville in Amsterdam, in which he was warned to be
prepared to receive him, that Crammon received another
letter from London which came actually via Brussels, and
that this latter contained suggestions for making a
separate Peace between France and England ; that these
suggestions came from the Duke of Newcastle and from
Lord Granville ; that this letter had been communicated
to him by Mme de Pompadour (he gave details . . .
" she was in bed ") ; that her delight was great, she told
him to mention it to Choiseul ; that he remonstrated but
ended by obeying ; that Choiseul rejected everything.
. . . Concerning Amsterdam, St. Germain spoke of its
greatness, of the number of its inhabitants, its treasures,
its money circulation, its superiority in this respect to
London, Paris and any other city in the world."

Tuesday, March 11th, 1760.

He told me that he had informed Mme de Pompadour
of what had passed between himself and me . . . and
that he had also written to the Minister to that effect.
When I asked him how the Minister would receive the
news, he said with a smiling but assured look that changes
would be soon taking place at Versailles, giving me to

understand that it would not be in Choiseul's power to prevent Peace for long.

Wednesday, March 12th, 1760.

That he had spoken to d'Affry on the subject of myself, and had told him that he would do wrong and fail in his duty to his master if he neglected me.

Sunday, March 16th, 1760.

The whole of the conversation was so varied and so full of extraordinary anecdotes, together with the singularity of the man himself and other circumstances (which I, however, knew already more particularly from Yorke and d'Affry), dealing with his relations with the King and Mme de Pompadour, that it occurred to me to take advantage of it in order to fathom the depths of this business, and thus forestall the false information of various people engaged in it who are only thinking of their own interests, put right the wrong impressions which are rife as to the policy of this Country, and insinuate myself into an affair which it is most important that I should understand clearly, despite the inclination which is shown to exclude me from it. In pursuance of this plan I egged him on by my queries to which he replied promptly and clearly. . . . (He speaks like a mere " rattlepate," although I would not venture to say that he is one.) I evinced great impartiality for all nations except my own ; professed to desire Peace for humanitarian reasons alone, and to share the personal grief of the King with regard to the condition of the French Nation, of which he (St. Germain) gave me a vivid and detailed picture, as that of a man who knew more than others on this subject. He spoke with so much precision of people, that I went on as I had begun and told him of my hopes, of the silly rumours and the absurd and ridiculous stories which the foreign Ministers here wrote to their masters. . . . I egged him on, making him speak (which is easy enough !) and he continued smoothly. . . .

Wednesday, March 26th, 1760.

. . . That he had decided on Monday to call on d'Affry, who told him that he had received letters from Versailles ordering him to tell him (St. Germain) that he had *got himself into a bad scrape at Court* by writing about me to Mme de Pompadour, *into a bad scrape indeed !* That he mixed himself up far too much with things which did not concern him ! And that he (St. Germain) was ordered in the King's name to mind his own business ! That d'Affry had spoken as if he thought he could scare him into leaving the place ; that he had also told him he had orders not to see him (St. Germain), but to deny him admittance !

Listening to him to the end, he (St. Germain) had finally answered that " if anyone had got into a bad ' scrape ' it was not himself but d'Affry . . . that as regards what had been enjoined on him in the name of the King, he (St. Germain), not being his subject, the King could not *order* him to do anything ; that moreover he believed that M. de Choiseul had written it all on his own initiative and that the King knew nothing about it ! If he were shown an order (written) by the King himself he would believe it : but not otherwise. . . ." He (St. Germain) told me that he had written an " Instructive Memoir " which he intended to send d'Affry and which he read aloud to me. He laughed and I did the same, thinking of the effect that his " Instructive Memoir " would have on d'Affry. He called the latter " block-

head," " poor fellow " and " this poor d'Affry who thinks
he can awe and bully me, *but . . . he has come to the
wrong person, for I have trampled under foot both praise
and blame, fear and hope, I, who have no other object but
to follow the dictates of my benevolent feelings towards
humanity and to do as much good to mankind as possible.
The King knows very well that I fear neither d'Affry nor
M. de Choiseul.*"

Thursday, March 27th, 1760.

The Comte de St. Germain told me under pledge of
secrecy, as " he did not wish to conceal anything from
me," that he had spent this day four hours with M.
Yorke, who had shown him the answers that he had received from England on the 25th, dated the 21st, from
the Duke of Newcastle, Mr. Pitt and Lord Holdernesse,
relating to what Yorke had written them about his previous conversations with him (St. Germain). He thereupon showed me three little notes which he had received
and which he made me read ; in one of these notes Yorke
expressed the wish to talk with him and specified what
was required from the Comte in order that they might
speak with one another without being disavowed in their
public or private positions . . . it was demanded that he
(St. Germain) should be " officially empowered " or something akin to that, in order that it might be possible for
York to speak openly with him, without fear of being
compromised.

He (St. Germain) told me that Yorke had given him
the original letters of the before-named ministers to read ;
that he knew the handwriting of each of them except
that of Pitt, and that these letters were most complimen-
tary to him. . . .

. . . Do what he might, d'Affry was now powerless,

and he (St. Germain) held the question of Peace in his own hands ; the only remaining obstacle in his way was M. de Choiseul who might " perhaps fail to extract all the benefit possible for Europe in general and France in particular from this opportunity."

Upon this I told him he should find some device wherewith to control M. de Choiseul's actions. He asked for my opinion (just as if *I* knew the French Court and the strong and weak points of the people in it !). I said it " was for him to find any such means," etc. . . . he seemed to be anxious about the reply he would get from Choiseul, whom he dared not ignore but whose real desire for Peace he strongly doubted. . . .

Monday, March 31st, 1760.

. . . He told me he possessed something which would " knock Choiseul into a cocked hat," that all decent people in France desired Peace . . . that Choiseul alone wished to continue the war . . . that he had a powerful weapon against Choiseul in the letters which Yorke had written him, and of which he kept the originals to use if necessary against Choiseul whom he did not fear in the least . . . that d'Affry was the slave of Choiseul . . . that Choiseul would not dare to conceal letters of which Mme de P. and the Marshal de Belle-Isle were informed.

Friday, April 14th, 1760.

Councillor Pensionnaire (Stein) told me that d'Affry had informed him that the orders he had received from Choiseul with regard to St. Germain consisted mainly in disavowing everything that St. Germain had done or would do here, with regard to the Peace . . . that by them he was obliged to communicate this to St. Germain adding that if he mixed himself up in the matter he would be imprisoned on his return to France. . . . The Recorder Fagel said to me much the same thing as that which " had told him only this morning." . . . The same day St. Germain dined with me and told me that " d'Affry had communicated his orders to him and shown him Choiseul's letter " ; he had answered that this " would not hinder him from returning to France, that these orders would never be put into force . . . that they only emanated from Choiseul . . . that he had known Yorke from his childhood, 17 years back, and that the Yorke family had always been kindness itself to him " ; . . . that d'Affry had also objected to his frequently calling upon me, which St. Germain had owned to doing and had added that he " intended to continue doing so." That d'Affry had shewn him Choiseul's letter together with the one that he (St. Germain) had himself written about me to Mme de Pompadour (to this he added that he was convinced that Choiseul had stolen it from Mme de P.) ; also that d'Affry had repeatedly told him that France would never trust me. . . . On the whole it seemed as if he cared very little for the orders which d'Affry had received with regard to him, and still less for M. de Choiseul ! . . . and that the whole matter remained undecided ; . . . that France would run the risk of War again and that if such a thing happened he (St. Germain) would " go to England and then see what he could do."

Tuesday, April 15th, 1760.

The Councillor Pensionnaire told me, in his room, that d'Affry had shown him the orders that he had received the night before by a courier declaring that St. Germain was a " mere vagabond," and that everything that he might have said should be disowned ! That a complaint should be drawn up against him, that he should be arrested and brought under escort to Lille to be handed over to France where he would be imprisoned. . . . I told him my view, which was that St. Germain had come to this country like other strangers trusting in the protection of the Law and counting on his safety as one of the public ; that he was not charged with any crime of such a nature that no Sovereign would give protection against it, such as murder, poisoning, etc., and that the right of sanctuary was considered very sacred in this Republic. . . . He agreed to this, but seemed very anxious about the feelings of France. . . . I went into the Recorder's room and he told me in the presence of the Councillor Pensionnaire, that d'Affry had come to him and told him . . . (follows the same discourse as with the Coun. Pen.), . . . and that he had advised him to address himself to the Government etc. ; . . . but that he did not think that the Government would hand over a person who lived in this country trusting to its protection, and against whom there was no charge of any heinous crime against which no Sovereign would grant protection. . . .

Wednesday, April 16th, 1760.

" . . . I told the Councillor Pensionnaire that M. de St. Germain had gone, of which he seemed very glad. . . ."

Wednesday, April 16th, 1760.

When I informed Yorke of what I had just heard about St. Germain I expected that he would shield him, for Yorke had begun to negociate with St. Germain and had encouraged him ; I have myself seen the originals of his letters to St. Germain, they are very friendly and encouraging. But, instead of shielding St. Germain, Yorke put on his hard, haughty and supercilious expression saying that he " would be very glad to see St. Germain in the hands of the Police." I was thunderstruck, knowing what I did : I told him my opinion, very gently and diffidently so as not to offend him ; but Yorke persisted in saying that " he washed his hands of St. Germain," and refused to let me have a passport for the Packet Boat which I had asked him to give me.

Pressed by me, Yorke said at last that if *I* asked him for a passport, as a *personal* favour, he would not refuse me " owing to my position." I agreed ; . . . mentioned that d'Affry might cause us a lot of trouble which might be prevented by giving St. Germain the means to escape, and Yorke then called his Secretary and bade him bring a passport. He signed it and handed it to me " blank," so that St. Germain might fill in his own name or whatever other name he might choose to take in order to avoid the pursuit of d'Affry or his minions. I carried away the passport without showing Yorke to what an extent I was shocked and revolted by what I had witnessed.

Thursday, April 17th, 1760.

The Councillor Pensionnaire writes to tell me that d'Affry called on him in order to complain of me ; that d'Affry said he was well informed of everything, that I had gone to see the Comte de St. Germain on Tuesday evening about 10, and had stayed with him until one hour after midnight, that a coach drawn by four horses had arrived before the house with a servant of mine and that M. de St. Germain had left in this coach with my servant behind, and that he (d'Affry) was consequently unable to fulfil his instructions !

April 18th, 1760.

Some months ago Mr. Yorke recommended to me very warmly a certain Mr. Linières who came here in order to

secure a patent for a machine of new invention. . . .
D'Affry paid me a visit, and while speaking of Linières
mentioned that he was connected with St. Germain. The
name struck me and excited my curiosity on account of
all that I had heard about the Count in England, where
he had stayed a considerable time and mixed in the best
Society. No one knew who he was, a fact which did not
astonish me in a country like England, where there are
practically no secret police, but what did astonish me was
that in France it was not known either ! D'Affry told me
that in France the King alone knew it, and in England
he believed the Duke of Newcastle knew it also. I
repeated to M. d'Affry several particulars which I had
heard about St. Germain concerning his manners, wealth
and magnificence, the regularity with which he paid his
debts, the large sums he had spent in England where life
is expensive, etc. M. d'Affry observed that he was
decidedly a very remarkable man of whom all kinds of
stories were told, each more absurd than the other : for
instance that he possessed the Philosopher's Stone, that
he was a hundred years old, altho' he did not look like
forty, etc. ! Having asked him if he knew him personally
he answered " yes," that he had met him at the house of
the Princesse de Montaubon, that he was a very welcome
and well-known figure at Versailles and often called on
Madame de Pompadour, that he was exceedingly sump-
tuous and magnificent, . . . and amongst other things
gave me particulars of his munificence with regard to
paintings, jewels and curios ; he told me still more which
I do not remember, nor do I remember all the questions
I put him. . . .

Pondering over what occurred between the Comte
d'Affry and myself, I have the impression that he was
as astonished as I was myself at these particulars with

regard to the figure which the Comte de St. Germain had cut in England and in France being discussed without a single imputation being made against him. . . .

I will mention this in the course of conversation with Yorke. . . .

Yorke spoke of him as being a *very cheerful and very polite man, who had insinuated himself into the cabinet of Mme de Pompadour and to whom the King had given Chambord*. . . .

He mentioned that later on, he made St. Germain's acquaintance when the latter had been in Amsterdam and came to the Hague. . . . It was in March he (St. Germain) came to see me owing to what Linières had written him [viz. that Bentinck van Rhoon wished to make his acquaintance] ; . . . his conversation pleased me very much, being exceedingly brilliant, varied and full of details about various countries he had visited . . . all very interesting. . . . I was exceedingly pleased with his judgment of persons and places known to me ; his manners were exceedingly polite and went to prove that he was a man brought up in the best society. He had come from Amsterdam with Madame *Geelvinck* and Mr. *A. Hope* and had been admitted daily to the house of *Mayor Hasselaar ;* he had come to the Hague recommended to M. de Soele, by the Hasselaar family who had taken him to Mme de Byland and elsewhere. On the birthday of the Prince of Orange at the old Court (giving his name at the door) I took him to the Ball where he was spoken to by the Hasselaars, by Mme Geelvinck, Mme Byland and others.

It had been his intention to leave on the day after the Ball, and he had retained a coach from Amsterdam in order to drive home the two ladies who had come with him, but they made him stay three or four days longer.

During this time he was daily with d'Affry and dined at d'Affry's house before returning to Amsterdam ; I had several talks with him of which most have slipped from my memory. . . . It is noteworthy that during the interval which elapsed between the day after the Ball and the day on which he left, d'Affry (believing him to be about to start) sent wine and meat for the journey to St. Germain every day. I can bear witness to this myself, as I was present when d'Affry's servant brought them on two succeeding days.

As St. Germain did not leave after all, he went and dined at d'Affry's house. . . .

I went myself to the Comte de St. Germain and advised him in his own interests to leave as soon as possible. I told him I was informed, not directly, but thro' a third person, that d'Affry had instructions to order his arrest and to have him conducted under escort to the French frontier and given up to France, in order that he might be imprisoned there for the rest of his life.

He was exceedingly surprised, not so much at M. de Choiseul giving such an order, as at D'Affry daring to think of doing such a thing in a law-abiding country ; he put a lot of questions each one more pertinent than the other, and with the greatest composure in the world ; I did not wish to discuss the matter with him, as I should have found it rather difficult to answer his enquiries and enlighten him on the points he raised. I told him there was no time for discussion, but that he should start at once if he considered his safety, that he had till the morrow to make his preparations, as even if M. d'Affry intended to take steps he could not do so until 10 o'c. the next morning, and before then he (St. Germain) should have made and carried out his plans.

The method of his retreat was now discussed as well as the question of where to go. . . .

With regard to the first, I offered him my services . . . with regard to the second, I suggested England ; its proximity, its laws, its constitution and the greatness of this nation offering him a nearer and safer refuge than that of any other country. . . . We agreed on this point ; I said that I would procure him a passport from Mr. Yorke, as without it he could not embark on the Packet Boat. As a ship was crossing the next day, I said he would do well to go on board at Hellevoetsluis and to do so as quickly as possible ; this done all d'Affry's proceedings would be too late, etc. . . . In the evening about seven or eight o'clock I went to St. Germain and took him the passport. He put a lot of questions to me which I evaded answering, requesting him to think rather of more pressing matters than of queries which were abstruse and useless in the present emergency. He decided to leave : as none of his servants knew either the language or the roads or the customs of the country, he asked me to lend him one of mine, which I did, with pleasure. . . . I did more, I ordered a coach with four horses for the purpose of going to Leyden to be before my house at 4.30. next morning, and told one of my servants to pick up the Comte de St. Germain on the way and stay with him until he should be sent back to me. . . .

(*A defence of his* (*Bentinck's*) *conduct follows, saying that secret treaties have always been allowed.*)

If the Comte de St. Germain had shown as much prudence as he had shown zeal, he would have, I believe, much accelerated Peace ; but he relied too much on his own intentions and had not a bad enough opinion of those of the men with whom he had to deal. What piqued

Comte d'Affry was an underlined sentence in a letter which St. Germain wrote to Mme de Pompadour. (I have heard it from those who have seen it). . . . I have only to account for my conduct to God and my Sovereign . . . as to what goes on in my house . . . the people I see and admit, of these I need give no account. For thirty years I have been a member of the Nobility and I am known never to have mixed with adventurers or impostors, or to have received scoundrels. M. de St. Germain came here with very good recommendations, I saw him because I liked his company and conversation ; he is an agreeable and polite man whose conversation is amusing and varied ; one can see at a glance that he has been brought up in the very best Society : true I do not know who he is, but the Comte d'Affry told me that his Most Christian Majesty knows ; . . . that is enough for me ! Should M. de St. Germain return to the Hague I shall again see him, unless the States of Holland forbid it or unless I become convinced myself that he does not merit admittance to my house.

April 25th, 1760.

I have been told that St. Germain was at Dijon and lived there very sumptuously. The Comte de Tavannes, the Governor, wrote to the Court enquiring what policy to pursue with regard to him . . . as he " did not know who he was." . . . He got the reply that he was to show the Comte de St. Germain all the consideration due to a man of his position, and to permit him to live in his own fashion.

APPENDIX IV

EXTRACTS FROM THE " MEMOIRS OF HARDENBROCK "
(EDITION OF THE HISTORISCH GENOOTSCHAP OF
UTRECHT), VOL. I, P. 220; TRANSLATED FROM THE
DUTCH ORIGINAL.

April, 1760.

I have been told that Rhoon (Bentinck) had despicable
relations with the English, amongst whom there was a
certain Paymaster named Nugent, although the Comte de
St. Germain, who is away at present, considered him well
disposed towards France.

May, 1760.

Doublet told me the following, declaring he had heard
it from Hompesch : . . . " that Rhoon had several
secret interviews with the so-called Comte de St. Germain, after which the Comte de St. Germain called on the
French Ambassador telling him that Rhoon was not as
friendly disposed towards England as was believed ; that
he (St. Germain) had written to France to this effect and
that this being so, such an influential man should be made
use of." D'Affry finally answered the repeated entreaties
of the Comte de St. Germain by saying that he " knew the
Sieur Rhoon well ; who, being dependent on England as
he was, could not render services of any value to France."
He (d'Affry) consequently requested him (St. Germain)
no longer to frequent his house.

Upon this followed the demand of France for the arrest of the Comte de St. Germain. He was however warned and left . . . in a carriage with one of Rhoon's servants, armed with a passport which Rhoon had procured him, by the help of the Minister Yorke. The latter, however, would only give it in " blank," and Rhoon filled in the name himself, repeatedly saying that the move on the part of France was nothing but " Court intrigue."

March 20th, 1762.

I have been told that the so-called Comte de St. Germain has now taken up his residence at UBBERGEN near NIMEGUE ; that he also owns some landed property near Zutphen ; that he has a huge laboratory in his house in which he shuts himself up for whole days at a time ; that he knows how to bestow the most lovely colours imaginable on things, for instance on leather, etc. ; that he is a great philosopher and lover of Nature ; a fine conversationalist ; that he seems to be virtuous ; that he looks like a Spaniard of high birth ; that he speaks with much feeling of Madame his late mother ; that he sometimes signs himself " prince d'Es." . . . ; that he is proud that he is desirous of encouraging Manufactures in the Republic, but that it is not his intention to favour any one town or Province, in spite of the fact that Amsterdam has already made advantageous offers to him on condition that other places should be excluded ; that he has rendered great services to Gronsveld by helping him to prepare the colours for his China Factory in Weesp ; that he is on the best of terms with Rhoon, on whom he often calls and with whom he corresponds ; that he has besides an enormous correspondence with foreign countries ; that he is known at every Court ; that the late Prince of Wales (who was a despicable character) treated him very badly, but that he (St. Germain) being innocent was again set free and rehabilitated ; that he corresponds with most important people in France ; that he speaks very highly of Mme de Pompadour, etc.   He often goes to Amsterdam, where he has called several times on G. Hasselaar ; he possesses precious stones of singular beauty : rubies, sapphires, emeralds and diamonds.   It is said that he knows how to impart the lustre of those of first water to *all* diamonds, and how to give the stones more brilliant colours.   He is very generous, he owns large properties in the Palatinate and in other parts of Germany ; in Amsterdam he takes up his quarters sometimes at other places, and he pays well everywhere.

APPENDIX V

CATALOGUE DES OUVRAGES IMPRIMÉS ET MANUSCRITS COMPOSANT LA BIBLIOTHÈQUE MAÇONNIQUE DU GRAND ORIENT DE FRANCE, 1882.

N. 498.

Régistre de la Loge du Contrat Social de St. Jean d'Ecosse, ci-devant de l'Equité et antérieurement de Saint-Lazare, depuis 18 Août 1775—19 Janvier 1789.

Manuscrits avec les signatures de :

> Pasquier
> de Saint-Germain
> Lord Elech
> Brognard
> Rousseau
> Président de la Garde
> Ségur
> Montesquiou
> Ger. de Saint George
> Teudon
> Grimaldi Monaco
> et beaucoup d'autres.

(Document considérable relatant des faits inconnus,

et indiquant l'esprit qui se produisait dans l'institution.

Les noms de St. Lazare, Equité et Contrat Social que la Loge a portés indiquent la marche des idées alors.)

(Extrait par L. A. Langeveld, Paris 31 Mai 1906.)

APPENDIX VI

ADDITIONAL MITCHELL PAPERS, VOL. XV. LORD HOLDER-
NESSE'S DESPATCHES, ETC., 1760. 6818, PLUT. P. L.
CLXVIII., 1 (12).

(BY BLACKMORE)

Hble. Maj. Gen. Yorke.

(Secret.)

Whitehall, March 21st, 1760.

Sir,

His Majesty commands me to acquaint you, that you
are at liberty to read my secret letter of this date to
Count de St. Germain as often as he desires it, and even
to let him take such precautions as he may think necessary to assist his Memory, in order to avoid all mistakes,
in conveying His Majesty's sentiments to the Court of
France. HOLDERNESSE.

Right Honourable Earl of Holdernesse.

(Secret.)

The Hague, March 25th, 1760.

My Lord,

I received this afternoon by Blackmore, the messenger,
the honour of your Lordship's secret letter of the 21st
instant ; it is unnecessary perhaps for me to say that His
Majesty's gracious approbation of my conduct, in my
conversation with Count St. Germain, was a great con-
solation to me, and I return your Lordship my humble

thanks for the early information you have been so good as to give me of it, for you will easily imagine some anxiety must attend the touching upon such delicate points.

As I have now His Majesty's clear and ample instructions, I shall lose no time in carrying them into execution, and have taken measures this evening to let M. St. Germain know at Amsterdam, that I had some particulars to acquaint him with in consequence of our former interview. I shall not fail to explain very clearly what your Lordship prescribes, and endeavor to bring him still closer to the point than I thought it decent to insist upon before I knew His Majesty's sentiments ; of all that passes your Lordship shall be immediately informed, and in the meanwhile I have the honour to remain with the greatest respect. . . . JOSEPH YORKE.

Hon. Gen. Yorke.

(Secret.)

Whitehall, March 28th, 1760.

Sir,

His Majesty is of opinion, as well from the tenor of your several letters, as by other advices that have been received, that the Duc de Choiseul is the least inclined to pacific measures of any of those who are in credit at the Court of Versailles ; and this in consequence of his predilection for the alliance of the House of Austria ; but that finding the pacific party too prevalent to be openly withstood, he has acquiesced in authorising Mr. d'Affry to talk in the manner he has done, in order, at least, to have a share in the negociation for peace, if that measure shall ultimately be determined, or to delay or disappoint the measure itself, which he has endeavoured to do, by naming a person whom he imagined could not be accepted here, and by even delaying the departure of that person, till the arrival of Mr. de Fuentes, which cannot be in less than two months. But notwithstanding the notion which is entertained of Mons. de Choiseul's intentions, the King thinks it proper that the overture made by Mr. d'Affry should not be discouraged, but that pretty much the same answer should be returned to him as has already been given to Mr. St. Germain, as you will observe by my other letter of this date, there being no other difference but what relates to the new hint thrown out by Mr. d'Affry, of sending a person to London. You will observe, the King has no objection to it, if a proper person is chosen, but His Majesty is determined not to receive one of his own subjects in quality of negotiator from France, and of all others, Mr. Dunn would be the most unfit for such a commission, and most obnoxious here. The precedent of Mr. Wall is not analogous to the present case ; but were it so, His Majesty would still be at liberty to make this exception. It still appears to His Majesty probable enough that Count St. Germain was authorised to talk to you in the manner he has done, and that his commission is unknown to the Duc de Choiseul : but as that minister will, in all likelihood, communicate the answer returned to Mr. d'Affry to a formal proposal, made, by order of his Court, to those persons who have employed St. Germain, His Majesty thought proper that there should be an exact uniformity in the answers given to both ; as it is not the King's intention to neglect either of these channels, you will therefore seek the earliest opportunity of having an interview with Mr. d'Affry ; and as my other letter is wrote in an ostensible manner, you may read it all to him, and even suffer him to take a note of what is underlined in it.

HOLDERNESSE.

To the Earl of Holdernesse.

(Secret.)

The Hague, March 28th, 1760.

My Lord,

Count St. Germain came to me yesterday morning in consequence of my having acquainted him of my being desirous to speak to him ; I was very free in explaining to him the impossibility there was of entering any farther into conversation with him, without he could produce an authentic authority from, or in the name of, His Most Christian Majesty, for negotiating upon the affair, which had made the subject of our last conversation. I told him that I was avowed and he was not, and therefore all he said might be disavowed at once ; whilst what came from me would bear the respectable mark of the character the King honoured me with. I was as strong as possible upon this point, by way of introduction to the communication I had leave to make to him, by the orders contained in your Lordship's *secret* letter of the 21st inst. ; and added that, though it was evident there was more than one opinion at the Court of France, yet, we could not treat with different persons, some of whom were authorized and some not : that, as he knew the public step the King had made, in opening a congress to His enemies, and since that, the unprecedented mark of generosity His Majesty had showed in permitting me to enter into *pourparlers* with M. d'Affry, it was needless to expatiate upon the inutility and impropriety of farther measures on our part, if he did not meet with a proper return.

Having premised this, I told him that out of regard to the person whose letters he had communicated to me formerly, and from conviction that he was sincere in desiring to advance so salutary a work, I had the King's permission to communicate to him His Majesty's further sentiments about a reconciliation with the Court of France : which ought to convince every well-meaning person how sincere and how pure His Majesty's sentiments are.

I accordingly communicated to him your Lordship's despatch, and at his desire permitted him to minute down the latter part of it : *It is therefore His Majesty's pleasure*, to the end.

Thus as we went in consequence of my orders ; but as an incident had happened since my last letter in relation to Count St. Germain, which M. d'Affry (who knows nothing as yet of his conversation with me) had talked of very freely, I was desirous to know how he told the story, which is as follows : On Sunday, M. d'Affry received a courier from the Duc de Choiseul, with orders to say that M. St. Germain was charged with nothing from the Court of France, that he (d'Affry) should let him know, that he should not frequent his house and even forbid him to come there.

This M. d'Affry acquainted St. Germain with, on Wednesday, upon his waiting upon him in the name of the French King ; but upon the latter's desiring to see the order, because he could not imagine it came from His Most Christian Majesty, M. d'Affry retracted that part and said it was not absolutely from the King, but from the Duc de Choiseul, as Secretary for Foreign Affairs. This was accompanied with great protestations of regard, and at the same time, a desire to have some further conversation with him the next day, which St. Germain declined, as unwilling to expose the Ambassador to any second breach of orders, which he had already broke thro', by letting him in. M. d'Affry let drop, that this order was occasioned by a letter St. Germain had wrote to Mme de Pompadour, which as he phrased it, *lui avait fait une diable d'affaire à Versailles*, tho' he denied knowing anything of the contents of the letter. St. Germain appealed to the proofs he had given him upon his arrival, of his not being unavowed, declared his being perfectly easy about the effect of any letter he had wrote, and in a manner set the Ambassador at defiance, and took leave of him abruptly ; notwithstanding which M. d'Affry sent after him again yesterday, and exprest his uneasiness at not having seen him, fearing he might be indisposed ; whether he has been there since, I don't know. This new episode in the romance of Count St. Germain did not much surprise me, nor should I wonder, tho' he pretends to fear nothing, if some time or other a powerful French Minister puts a stop to his travelling. I was, however, curious to know what he proposed to do, in consequence of it, and in what manner to proceed, in the business he had undertaken. Here I think, for the first time, I caught him wavering a little : whether that proceeded from any apprehension of the Duc de Choiseul's resentment, or from what he pretends, the indifference for business on the part of the French King, and the indecision of the Lady, I won't pretend to say : but I found him in some doubt, whether he should not work, to bring the Duc de Choiseul himself, with the system he supposed to be revelled in the breasts of those in whose names he speaks.

It was not my business to lead him in such an affair, and therefore I only threw out that that seemed to me a delicate affair at a distance, and might embarrass those who protected him. I pushed him after that to inform me in what manner he intended to make use of what I had leave to show him, and whether he intended to go himself to Versailles. This he declined for the present, as he said, he might be sent back again immediately, and should only give more umbrage ; but he would send a servant of his with three letters, one to marshal Belleisle, one to Mme de Pompadour, and a third to the Comte de Clermont, Prince of the Blood, whom he mentioned for the first time, as his intimate friend, and as one, who had the French King's confidence, independently of his ministers, and who was a fast friend to the coming to an immediate accommodation with England. To remove all suspicion of his deceiving me, he did, in reality, produce a letter from that Prince to him, of the 14th inst., wrote in the most friendly and cordial terms, lamenting his absence, and wishing strongly for his speedy return. From the two last mentioned persons he made no doubt of receiving answers ; from Mme de Pompadour, he did not, he said, expect it, because it was a maxim with her, not to *write* upon state affairs, tho' it was absolutely necessary to inform her, that he was strengthened, and able to work on her side.

All this is very plausible, but the effect is still to be proved. In the meantime, it is plain, that these French ministers counteract each other, and consequently are in different systems ; which is to prevail, don't depend upon us, but it can't be deterimental to His Majesty's service, that his sentiments should be known to the Court of France, by any channel they think fit to receive them thro'.

M. d'Affry's compliments, after his acquainting St. Germain with the Duc de Choiseul's orders, are as extraordinary as the rest, especially as he knows very well his connexion with marshal Belleisle, and had seen the French King's passport to him. All this mystery will be unveiled by degrees, and I shan't fail to inform your Lordship of the further lights I can collect ; I let Mr.

St. Germain know that he or any other person, duly authorised, was equal in England, the chief objection we had at present, and what stopt the whole, was the want of a proper and sufficient credential. . . .

JOSEPH YORKE.

To the Earl of Holdernesse.

(Secret.)

The Hague, April 8th, 1760.

My Lord,

It is rather to show my attention to all the material letters your Lordship honoured me with, on the 28th past, than from anything very particular I have to trouble you with, that I take the liberty to acknowledge by themselves the honour of your Lordship's *secret* letters of that date, and of the 1st instant.

I must acquaint you, however, that I spoke very plainly to Mr. d'Affry upon the subject of Mr. Dunn . . . and explained to him in the strongest and fullest manner why it would be impossible to receive him as a negotiator from the Court of France.

I must do the French Ambassador the justice to say, that he entered into the reasons alleged, but endeavoured to persuade me that the Duc de Choiseul could not mean to propose a man, whom he had not conceived a good opinion of ; but that he hoped upon the representations he should now make to him, in form, that that would be waived.

Mr. St. Germain is still at the Hague, but has not as yet produced anything new from France, and it is highly probable that after the noise his first letters made, nobody will care to risk a direct correspondence with him, which may cross the Duc de Choiseul's measures ; Mr. d'Affry pretends that that French Minister is desirous of Peace, because His Most Christian Majesty is, and that it is serving his Master according to his wishes. Indeed, the reserve the French Ambassador observes towards the Ministers of their Allies here, the awkward uneasiness he shewed lest they should know we had met, and several expressions he let drop about them and their Courts, would incline me to think, that Peace is the object of France, and that the pacific party is the most prevalent : but for the proof of that we must wait for the answer to the Communication I have just made, which is so fair and so confidential, that if they don't come into it, there cannot remain the least doubt here-after of their determination to try the fate of the Campaign.

I am infinitely obliged to your Lordship for encourag-ing me with the assurance of His Majesty's approbation of my conduct, and I humbly recommend myself to the indulgence of His Majesty and of His Servants, in the course of this delicate affair. . . .

JOSEPH YORKE.

From Mr. Mitchell to Lord Holdernesse.

Head Quarters at Freyburg,
Thursday, March 27th, 1760.

My Lord,

Twice I had the honour of your Lordship's Courier of the 4th by Badmore, and of the 14th by a Prussian Courier ; I have communicated the same to His Prussian Majesty's friendship, and unreserved confidence. He said he would follow the King's example. . . .

The King of Prussia thinks, that nothing certain can be concluded from all that has passed between Gen. Yorke and the French Ambassador, to the 4th inst., but he added he was in daily expectation of hearing something from France, that might be depended upon ; that he already had had accounts, that the person sent from the Court of Gotha had been well received : that the Bailli de Froulay, immediately upon reading his letter, went to Versailles ; and that he had promised to the emissary, to procure him a permission for sending of expresses and couriers and passports for himself to return, when it should be thought proper : he concluded with saying that so soon as he had any certain notice of what was passing at *Paris*, he would send a courier directly to England.

The King of Prussia was pleased then to give me some account of a most extraordinary conversation, which Count St. Germain had had with General Yorke, on the 15th, at the Hague, the particulars of which need not be mentioned, as your Lordship will have them more authentically : he observed that though the manners were of the most uncommon kind, yet Gen. Yorke had done . . . to give your Lordship an immediate account of what had passed, that it was very probable the Count may have been employed in this secret commission by the marshal Belleisle, without the knowledge of the other French Ministers as the Cabinet is extremely divided. He asked me if I was acquainted with this St. Germain, who, as he was informed, had been some time in England. I answered I had seen him there, but did not imagine he would ever become a negotiator. His Prussian Majesty answered that he heard the Count had found a way to insinuate himself into the good graces of the French King, whom he had amused with some experiments in Chemistry, and that the French King had made him a present of the *Château de Chambord*.[1]

A. MITCHELL.

[1] Compare with Appendix I.

Letter from Mr. Mitchell to Lord Holdernesse.

Freyburg, April 9th, 1760.

My Lord,

His Prussian Majesty mentioned me a letter from Monsieur de Bouillé, lately intercepted, in which that minister says that the French Court are inclined to peace ; that the disputes in Canada will be settled to the liking of the English ; to whom, likewise, Minorca will be restored, and Cape Breton to the French, but he hesitates much about the cession of Guadeloupe. He also said that Count d'Affry had, by order of the Duc de Choiseul, disavowed to the allied ministers, everything that Count St. Germain had said to General Yorke ; and that the Court of Vienna, at the solicitation of the French Ambassador, had at last consented to send Ministers to the congress ; but Kaunitz hinted they should be empowered to do nothing.

A. MITCHELL.

APPENDIX VII

MISCELLANEOUS PAPERS FROM ENGLISH RECORD OFFICE.

Some of these letters contain passages in cipher, with the writing as here given between the lines. The cipher is composed of a series of numerals, and may of course contain direct contradictions of the written words. But since the cipher of that period is changed, and the key is necessarily only known to those who have the charge of these affairs, it is impossible to burden the pages with useless matter.

Extract from a letter from M. Kauderbach.

(Rec. March 20th, 1760).

The Hague, March 14th, 1760.

To Prince Galitzin.

The courier of M. de Reischach has at last returned, but he has not brought the answer so anxiously expected. This minister must receive his orders from the Count de Stahremberg at Paris, just like the Count de Beschicheff. These gentlemen expect to receive them in two or three days. So we shall soon see what will be the end of this great affair.

It is singular that we cannot ascertain whether England will really send a body of troops to Germany, and of what strength it will be. It is said that the King of Prussia and Prince Ferdinand earnestly request this transport, but that they are not hurrying themselves about it in London.

We have here a very singular man. It is the celebrated
Count de St. Germain, known throughout Europe for his
learning and his immense wealth. He is charged with an
important commission in this country, and he talks much
of saving France by different means from those formerly
used by the famous Maid of Orleans. We must see how
he will set about it. He has a store of precious stones of
the greatest beauty. He claims to have snatched from
Nature her highest secrets and to know her throughout.
But the most curious thing is that he is said to be over
110 years of age ; he looks, however, not more than 45.
Gaudeant bene nati. I wish I could get at his secret for
your benefit, monsieur, and for my own also ! He is a
warm supporter of Mme de Pompadour and of the
marshal de Belleisle ; and he detests the two brothers
Paris, to whom he attributes all the misfortunes of
France. He talks very freely of all that concerns this
kingdom—from king to clown.

The letters from Germany have brought us nothing new.

Copy of a letter from M. Kauderbach.

(Rec. March 25th, 1760).

The Hague, March 19th, 1760.
To Prince Galitzin.

You will already have seen, monseigneur, the List of
the Prussian Armies which a courier has brought to
London, and which has also been communicated to M.
Verelat at Berlin. The King of Prussia at the same time
offers to verify its reality by causing a review of these
forces to be held before Mr. Mitchell. After this offer,
how can the English Parliament fear to throw itself
headlong into the projects of His Prussian Majesty and
to support him vigorously until his work is done and he
can turn to something else ?

If you have read the Philosopher of Sans Souci, you will find like many others that he keeps his foremost desires always at the bottom of his heart.   This abominable work, which the Prussians extol as the master-piece of the human intellect, has been blasted and anathematised as it deserves from the pulpits of Amsterdam, and has caused many enthusiasts to open their eyes to the fine principles of their Gideon.   Others carry their blindness to the further point, and persist in looking on this production as a forgery by his enemies.

We are still awaiting the famous Reply, of which, it is said, the only difficulty lies with France.   M. d'Affry received a courier on Thursday, but he says not a word of what he brought.   It would seem that he is waiting for something before sending him back, for he still retains him here.

I spoke to you in a former letter, monseigneur, of the famous St. Germain, who is at this moment in Amsterdam, where he is staying with Sieur Hoope.   He has seen Mr. Yorke at his house and remained there three hours. He has neither sent nor applied here to M. d'Affry and yet he told myself that he was charged with an important commission.   But, to tell the truth, he appears to me too presuming and too incautious to believe him to be a highly trusted negotiator.   I place him in the category with the famous Macanas, whom your Excellency knew here in 1747, or at least in that of the Count de Sekkendorff, who came here last year.   I shall be much mistaken in him if he succeeds in his commission.   Our Dutchmen are too thick-skulled to indulge in refinements. However, I have no longer any doubt that there are important negotiations on hand. . . . This man told me that France would cede Guadaloupe . . . if at this price she could obtain Peace ; . . . This would perhaps be no evil . . . if England abandoned Prussia to her own forces. . . . What do you think about it ? . . .

M. Wassemar informs me that the Count de Bristo. has had a long audience of the King of Spain, immediately after which he despatched a courier. All else is matter of speculation. Germany offers me nothing of interest to communicate, except the cruel and ceaseless sufferings of unhappy Saxony. The Prussians loudly declare that they will make it a desert. May God have mercy on this poor country.

Extract from the letter of Prince de Galitzin.
(*Rec. March 25th*, 1760.)

London, March 25th, 1760.

To M. de Kauderbach.

I know the Count de St. Germain well by reputation. This singular man has been staying for some time in this country, and I do not know whether he likes it. There is someone here with whom he appears to be in correspondence, and this person declares that the object of the Count's journey to Holland is merely some financial business. The gazettes and the people say that the King of Prussia reckoned on attacking the Austrians on the 25th inst. and the persons in office assert that this monarch will open the campaign with 150,000 men $\left(\begin{smallmatrix} m \\ 150 \end{smallmatrix} ?\right)$

It is certain that the Allies will muster in formidable strength this year in the campaign.

There is some likelihood that the unexpected death of the Count de Bestouchef may delay the reply in question ; though on the other hand, however, Prince de Galitzin, my first cousin, has already for some time past been authorised to remain as Minister to His Most Christian Majesty.

Copy of the letter from the Sieur Kauderbach.

(Rec. March 31st, 1760.)

(Decyphered.)

The Hague, March 28th, 1760.

To Prince Galitzin.

People here are talking more than ever of a private negotiation between England and France, and if one could judge by appearances one would be tempted to believe these reports had some foundation. I know for a certainty that Messrs. d'Affry and Yorke, after taking different routes in order to meet at the Bois, did effect an interview there. I know further that they have had a second similar meeting on the Ryswick Road. I leave you to judge what may be the reason for this affectation of conferring in public, and which of the two is most to the point.

The Prussians here say loudly that if the two Empresses do not lend themselves to Peace, France will go her own way. I hope that this may be only presumption on their part. M. de Reichach says " fear nothing " and he is sure of the harmony that reigns between his Court and France ; but I am not so easy as he is.

I have spoken to you of the Comte de St. Germain, who is here just now. M. d'Affry, after receiving him at his house where I have seen him in the best society, has just forbidden him the house, by order of his Court, and he has made this known to us. M. de St. Germain says that this order comes from M. de Choiseul, that he is reproached with having meddled with the affairs of the Peace, and that in fact he has made a report to Marshal Belleisle, from whom he shows letters full of confidence, of certain dispositions which he discovered in a conversation with M. Yorke ; that he also made it known that

M. d'Affry was too neglectful of a certain person of rank here, who appeared very well disposed. Indeed this story will make a sensation. It is certain that M. St. Germain has a passport signed by the King of France, which is very honourable to him, and in which mention is made of his mission to Holland. It is also sure that he was charged with a commission the result of which M. de Belleisle awaited with keen impatience, as is shown by one of his letters. Mme de Pompadour, of whom M. de St. Germain is a great apologist, is also mixed up with it. But it seems that this gentleman is not prudent enough with regard to M. d'Affry, and to tell the truth that gentleman did seem to me rather a fool. I entreat your Excellency to keep these particulars to yourself, for it is better that I should not mix myself up with these stories.

Your Excellency will see by the Leyden Gazette that the King of Prussia has, for urgent cause, just withdrawn the commissions of the Shipowners of Emden. That means something. The Swedish Minister here has told me that in England they have set completely at liberty, with an indemnification of a thousand pounds, a Swedish vessel captured by a Prussian armateur, and that the latter has been declared a privateer.

I add to this some remarkable writings of the philosopher of Sans Souci, and you will see what judgement is passed upon them in Switzerland. They have just accorded a kind of approbation to this book in Berlin, where it is to be reprinted by authority. It will be applauded by miscreants, but abhorred by all honest people, and the Supreme Being who is infamously outraged in it, will one day confound the impiety of its author and of those who give him their plaudits.

Copy of letter from Prince Galitzin.

(*Rec. April 1st, 1760.*)

London, April 1st, 1760.

To M. de Kauderbach.

I have read not without surprise the envenomed shaft of abominable impiety contained in fragments of the book in question, which you were kind enough to send me, although indeed nothing ought to surprise us on the part of this impious author. This latest production of his perverse mind is worthy of his odious sentiments. I shall be greatly obliged to you, monsieur, if you will kindly send me some time the whole of this book. I am not astonished that on the complaint of the Count de Galofkin the sale of this wretched book has been prohibited, but I am very much so that . . . dares to announce publicly the printing of such blasphemy ; and it seems to me that he may be made to repent of his boldness.

I am utterly ignorant of what foundation there is for speaking, with you, of a private negotiation between England and France. Here, we do not hear the slightest hint of such a thing, and if it were so, I should have been able to learn something of it. Those promenades spoken of in the Bois and at Reswyk do not appear of sufficient consequence to make one credit such rumours, telling at most only of presumption on one side and of imprudence on the other. Nevertheless, perfectly innocent as this conduct may be, it is, I venture to say, very much out of place under present circumstances. Still less can one approve of this eager and confident affectation of insinuating to the same persons that it is only owing to a certain court that a certain Reply, so much wished for, does not arrive. Insinuations of this kind, being all reported here, cannot remain unknown to the persons interested.

As to the language of the Prussians, it is well to pay no attention to it, and so all that they say about the two Empresses and France regarding the peace, is unworthy of consideration. All the world is equally anxious to conclude a peace, but a peace stable and honourable. The behaviour of the Count d'Affry by order of his court towards the Count de St. Germain who has emancipated himself from wishing to meddle with the affairs of the peace without the concurrence and participation of all the allied courts, sufficiently proved the falsity of the rumours which are current with you of a private negotiation, of which I have just spoken above. M. de St. Germain has everywhere been treated on the footing of an illustrious adventurer. Here, owing to his imprudence and his unguarded behaviour, he had been taken for a spy and treated accordingly. As for me, I, like yourself, think him somewhat of a fool.

You, monsieur, have better means than I have of knowing the truth of the article in the Leyden Gazette that you have sent me concerning His Majesty the King of Prussia, who has just withdrawn their commissions from the ship-owners of Emden. All that I know about it is that the Baron de Kniphausen formerly gave these commissions from the King his master to all the English who wished to sail over the seas under the Prussian flag. Commissions of this kind were sold here by an Englishman, who was no longer of a mind to make use of them himself, to another. One may easily guess what disorder these kinds of venality would produce. I do not know whether it was owing to the representations of certain courts, which you will easily guess and of which the Swedish minister ought no longer to be ignorant, or that justice alone has had the principal share in it, that these great abuses and disorders have been mentioned to

M. de Kniphausen, who has withdrawn several of these commissions of the King his master, and if not all of them as yet, it is to be believed that, the above-mentioned Leyden Gazette showing the true mind of His Prussian Majesty on this matter, the remainder of these instruments of pillage will be withdrawn forthwith.

M. de Kniphausen yesterday received a courier from the King his master, but up to the present he seems disposed to keep the contents of the despatch to himself. The courier also brought a letter from the King through his minister. . . .

Copy of letter from the Count Laurwig to the Count de St. Germain, at Paris.

Copenhagen, April 3rd, 1760.

My inclination would certainly have led me to continue the honour of your acquaintance by letter, when no longer happy enough to be able to see you. But I have not had the pleasure of knowing your address, and I did not venture to trouble you until the Chamberlain, the Baron de Gleichen, gave me the assurance that you honoured me with your remembrance. Accept this token of my gratitude and of the joy that I feel in having once more found an opportunity of thanking you for all the kindness and friendship with which you honoured me in England. The sword which you presented to me and the letters which you wrote to me, I have kept as a possession too valuable for me ever to part with ; but the honour of your remembrance of me is too deeply graven on my heart to allow me to lose this opportunity of assuring you of the profound esteem which is due to your dear self. Pray give me news of yourself and your commands if I can be of use to you in any way in this country ; and believe me, I am so rejoiced to find my friend again (allow me to use this term) that I know not how to express all my gratitude to you. Pray receive this letter kindly, and believe that it is with true pleasure that I can repeat that I am and shall be throughout my life. . . .

P.S. The address which is on this letter was given me by the Baron de Gleichen ; he told me that you wished to be written to in this way. Should you, my dear Count, honour me with a reply, my address is : Count de Danneskeold Laurwig, Knight Chamberlain and Admiral.

To the Comte de St. Germain, at the Hague.

(Extract.)

Amsterdam, April 27th, 1760.

If a thunderbolt had struck me, I could not have been more confounded than I was at the Hague when I found that you had left. I will play my last stake and make all conceivable efforts in the hope of being able to pay my respects to you in person, for I am well aware, Monsieur, that you are the greatest lord on earth ; I am only grieved that rascally people dare to give you trouble, and it is said that gold and intrigues are employed in opposition to your peaceful efforts. For the present I can breathe a little, for I am assured that M. d'Affry left suddenly on Thursday last for the Court and I hope from that that he will get what he deserves for having failed in what he owes to you, and I take him to be the cause of your long absence, and thus of my misfortune. If you find that I can be of use to you, count on my faithfulness ; I have nothing but my arm and my blood, but this is gladly at your service. THE COUNT DE LA WATÙ.

Copy of the letter of Mr. Cornet to the Count de Haslang.

The Hague, April 29th, 1760.

A foreigner who calls himself the Comte de St. Germain, whose origin and native country no one knows, but who is said to be extremely rich and very well received at different Courts in Europe, especially at that of France, after a residence of about three months which he has made here, has just disappeared when it was least expected. He has been intimately connected with the French Ambassador though he has been assiduous in seeing the Anglo-Prussian Ministers and partisans. Then, he has confided to some persons of distinction his correspondence with the Marshal Duc de Belleisle, who according to him was inclined to the re-establishment of peace between France and England, which he had in his pocket. The Count d'Affry made this known to the Duc de Choiseul who commanded him to see him no more and to threaten him with the Bastille if he continued to use such a language. The ambassador having given him this message in writing, the Count de St. Germain said publicly some days after that this minister had made enquiries about his health, that he had been extremely anxious about it and that he begged him to come and see him, the sooner the better ; but that he had excused himself, on the pretext that having regard to orders received from his own court, he would not risk it. This contradictory conduct on the part of the ambassador is attributed to an order that had come to him from the Duc de Belleisle, and is regarded as a clear proof of the little unanimity reigning between the two French Secretaries of State. However that may be, the Count de St. Germain continued to say that what he had asserted was exact truth. On a second report that the

Count d'Affry made on this to his Court, he was commanded to have him arrested and to demand his extradition to the King his master ; getting wind of which, M. de St. Germain departed first for Helvoet Sluys. As we know that the Count was in the good graces of the King and in regular correspondence with the Duc de Belleisle, people are generally persuaded that he was charged with some commission, and that his disgrace was caused either by his indiscretion, or by the want of union which is said to exist in the French ministry.

BIBLIOGRAPHY

ADHÉMAR (Comtesse d').—Souvenirs sur Marie-Antoinette. Paris, Mame ed., 1836.

ANSPACH (Margravine of).—Memoirs. London, 1826.

ARNETH (Alfred Ritter von).—Graf Philipp Cobenzl und seine Memoiren.

BARRUEL (l'Abbé).—Mémoires sur l'Histoire du Jacobinisme. Paris, 1797.

BARTHOLD (F. W. von).—Die geschichtlichen Persönlichkeiten in Jacob Casanova's Memoiren. Berlin, 1846.

BARTHOLD (F. W.).—Beiträge zur Geschichte des achtzehnten Jahrhunderts. Berlin, 1846.

BEAUJOINT (Jules).—The secret Memoirs of Madame la Marquise de Pompadour. London, 1885.

BEUGNOT (Comte de).—Mémoires. Paris, St. Germain, 1866.

BIESTER (Dr.).—Berliner Monatschrift. Berlin, 17....

BJÖRNSTAHL (J. J.).—Reise in Europa in 1774.

BLAVATSKY (H. P.).—Theosophical Glossary. London, 1892.

BLAVATSKY (H. P.).—Secret Doctrine, 3rd edition. London, 1893.

BLAVATSKY (H. P.).—Key to Theosophy, 3rd edition, London, 1893.

BOBÉ (Louis).—Johan Caspar Lavater's Reise til Danmark i Sommeren 1793. Copenhagen, 1898.

BOBÉ (Louis).—Papiers inédits de la famille de Reventlow, Copenhagen, 1898.

BUELAU (Prof. Friedrich).—Geheime Geschichten und räthselhafte Menschen ; Sammlung verborgener oder vergessener Merkwürdigkeiten.

CANTÙ (Cesare).—Gli Eretici d'Italia, Torino, 1868.

CANTÙ (Cesare).—Illustri Italiani, vol. II.

CAPENDU (Ernest).—Le Comte de St.-Germain. Paris, 1845.

CAPPONI (C.).—Memorie della famiglia Medici.

CASANOVA (F. Seingalt de).—Mémoires. Bruxelles, 1876.

CHALLICE (A. E. M.).—The secret History of the Court of France. London, 1861.

CLIFFORD (R.) (translator).—Memoirs illustrating the History of Jacobinism. London, 1797–8.

COBENZL (J. P.).—Graf P. Cobenzl. Wien, 1885.

CRÉQUI (La Marquise de).—Souvenirs. In " Bibliothèque Choisie " edited by M. Cousin.

DESCHAMPS (N.).—Les Sociétés Secrètes et la Société, ou Philosophie de l'Histoire Contemporaine, vol II. Paris, 1881.

DIDEROT.—Correspondance de Grimm et Diderot, Part III., vol. 3. Paris, 1829.

DUFORT (J. N. Comte de Cheverny).—Mémoires sur le règne de Louis XVI. Paris, 1886.

ECKERT (E. E.).—Magazin der Beweisführer für Verurtheilung des Freimaurer-Ordens, I., 137. Leipzig, 1857.

FREDERIC II.—De l'hiver de 1759 à 1760. Œuvres posthumes de Frederic II., roi de Prusse. Berlin, 1788.

FREDERIC II.—Œuvres Complètes de Frederic II. Berlin, 1790.

GASSICOURT (Cadet de).—Le Tombeau de Jacques de Molay. Paris, 1795.

GENLIS (Madame la Comtesse de).—Mémoires Inédites pour servir à l'Histoire des XVIII et XIX Siècles. Paris, 1825.

GLEICHEN (C. H. Baron de).—Mémoires. Paris, 1868.

GRAEFFER (Franz).—Kleine Wiener Memoiren. Wien, 1846.

GROSLEY (P. F.) (Membre de l'Académie des Inscriptions et Belles-Lettres de Londres).—Œuvres Inédites. Paris, 1813.

HASCHE (J. C.).—Diplomatische Geschichte, Dresden.

HAUGWITZ (Comte de).—Fragments de Mémoires inédites. Jena, 1830–1857.

HAUSSET (Madame du, femme de chambre).—Mémoires. Paris, 1824.

HESSE-CASSEL (Karl Prinz de).—Mémoires de mon temps. Copenhagen, 1861.

HEZEKIEL (Georg).—Abenteuerliche Gesellen. Berlin, 1862.

LAMBERG (Count Joseph Maximilian von).—Le Mémorial d'un mondain. Cap Corso, 1774.

LAMBERG (Mad. Jos. von).—Tagenbuch eines Weltmanns. Frankfurt am Main, 1775.

LE ROY (C. G.).—Louis XV. et Madame de Pompadour. Paris, 1876 (ed. by A. Poulet-Malassis).

LÉVI (Eliphas).—Histoire de la Haute Magie. Paris, 1860.

MAUVILLON (J.).—Geschichte Ferdinands, Herzog von Braunschweig-Lüneburg. Leipzig, 1794.

MAYNIAL (Edouard).—Casanova et son temps. Paris, 1911.

MENSEL (J. G.).—Vermischte Nachrichten und Bemerkungen. Erlangen, 1816.

MENU VON MINUTOLI.—Correspondence de Fréderic II. avec le Comte Algarotti. Berlin, 1837.

MINUTOLI (General-Lieutenant von).—Der Graf von Haugwitz, etc. Berlin, 1844.

MOUNIER (J. J.).—De l'Influence attribuée aux Philosophes, aux Francs-Maçons et aux Illuminés sur la Révolution de France. Tübingen, 1801.

NICOLAI (C. F.) (Editor).—Neue Allgemeine Deutsche Bibliothek, vol. 107. Stettin und Berlin, 1793–1806.

O'BYRN (F. A.).—Camillo, Graf Marcolini : Eine Biographische Skizze. Dresden, 1877.

OETTINGER (E. M.).—Graf St. Germain. Leipzig, 1846.

PATRIS-DEBREUIL (L. M.).—Œuvres Inédites de P. J. Grosley. Paris, 1813.

ST. GERMAIN.—A book of music composed by St. Germain. In the library of the Castle of Raudnitz in Bohemia, the property of Prince Ferdinand v. Lobkowitz.

ST. GERMAIN (attributed to).—Sonnet sur la Création. Poëmes Philosophiques sur l'Homme. Paris, Mercier, 1795.

SYPESTEYN (Cornelius Ascanius van).—Voltaire, St. Germain, etc. : Historische-Herinneringen. 's Gravenhage, 1869.

THIÉBAULT (Dieudonné).—Original Anecdotes of Frederick II. (trans. from French). London, 1805.

THIÉBAULT (Dieudonné).—Mes souvenirs de vingt ans de séjour à Berlin. Paris, 1813.

TOUCHARD-LAFOSSE (G.).—Chronique de l'Œil-de-Bœuf, des petits appartements de la Cour et des salons de Paris sous Louis XIV., la Régence, Louis XV. et Louis XVI. Paris, 1864.

VOLTAIRE (ed. by Beuchot).—Œuvres. Paris, 1829–40.

VULPUIS (C. A.) (Editor).—Curiositäten der physisch-literarisch-artistisch, etc. Weimar, 1811–23.

WALPOLE (Horace, Earl of Orford).—Letters to Sir Horace Mann. London, 1833.

WALPOLE (Horace).—George II. London, 1846.

WEBER (Dr. Carl von).—Aus vier Jahrhunderten. Mitteilungen aus dem Haupt-Staats-Archive zu Dresden. Tauchnitz, Leipzig, 1857.

WECKHELIN (W. L.).—Chronologien. Frankfurt am Main, 1779.

WRAXALL (Sir P. L.).—Memoirs of the Courts of Berlin, Dresden, Warsaw and Vienna in the years 1777, 78, 79. London, 1800.

WRAXALL (Sir P. L.).—Remarkable Adventures and unrevealed Mysteries. London, 1863.

ANONYMOUS AUTHORS :

— A few words about the first Helpers of Catherine II., Vol. XVIII. 1869.

— Le Comte de St. Germain et la Marquise de Pompadour par M..., auteur des Mémoires d'une femme de qualité et de la Duchesse de Fontange. Paris, 1838.

— Freimaurer Bruderschaft in Frankreich.

— Materials for the History of the Russian Literature. Edited by P. A. Efremoff, St. Petersbourg, 1867.

— Taschenbuch für Alchemisten, Theosophen und Weisensteinförscher, die es sind und werden wollen. Published by Christian Gottlieb Hilscher, Leipzig, 1790.

BIOGRAPHIES, ENCYCLOPÆDIAS, ETC.

— Allgemeine Encyclopädie by Ersch und Gruber. Leipzig, 1818 (sub voce).

—Bibliographie biographique. Ed. Oettingen, Leipzig, 1850 (sub voce).

— Genealogischer Archivarius. Historische Nachrichten aus dem Jahr 1734. Ed. M. Ranft, Leipzig.
— Grande Biographie Universelle du XIX Siécle. La rousse, Paris, 1825 (sub voce).
— Historisch-bibliographisches Buntoeler. F. Graeffer, Brünn, 1824 (sub voce).
— Meyer's grosse Konversations-Lexicon für die gebildeten Stände, vol. 7, p. 679. Hildburghausen, 1871–72.
— Oesterreichische National Encyclopädie. F. Gaeffer, Wien, 1835–37 (sub voce).
— Royal Masonic Cyclopædia. Mackenzie, London, New-York, 1877 (sub voce).

PERIODICALS

— All the Year Round. London, 1859.
— Berlinische Monatschrift. Band II., Berlin, June, 1785.
— Cornhill Magazine : " Historical Mysteries " by A. Lang. London, Nov. 1904.
— Gartenlaube : " Brause Jahre Bilder " von A. v. d. Elbe. Weimar, 1884. N. 38, 39.
— Gentleman's Magazine. April, 1760.
— Literarisches Wochenblatt der Börsenhalle, continued as Literarische Blätter der Börsenhalle. Hamburg, 1834, N. 914.
— London Chronicle, June 3rd, 1760.
— Neue Berlinische Monatschrift. Berlin und Stettin, Band 7, 8. 1802.
— Nineteenth Century. Jan. 1908.
— Notizie del Mondo. Florence, July, 1770.
— Once a Week. London, July 20th, 1861.
— Psychische Studien ; Monatliche Zeitschrift. Edited by A. Aksakof. Leipzig, 1885, p. 430.

— Read's Weekly Journal or British Gazetteer. May 17th, 1760.
— Revue des Deux Mondes : " Un Prince Allemand du XVIII Siècle " par St. René-Taillandier. Paris, Dec. 1865 et Fev. 1866.
— Revue Germanique. 30 Sept. 1860.
— Signatstern : oder die enthüllten sämmtlichen sieben Grade der mystischen Freimaurei, nebst dem Orden der Ritter des Lichts, etc. Vol. III., part I., vol. V., article 19. Berlin, 1804–09.
— Theosophist. May, 1881.
— Ueber Land und Meer ; Allgemeine Illustrirte Zeitung. Stuttgart, 1858.
— Zirkel. March 1st, 1908.